Health and Consciousness

through Fasting and Cleansing

By Dr. Nibodhi Haas

HEALTH AND CONSCIOUSNESS
through Fasting and Cleansing

By: Dr. Nibodhi Haas

Published by:
Mata Amritanandamayi Mission Trust
Amritapuri P.O., Kollam Dt, Kerala 690525, India
Websites: www.amritapuri.org
www.embracingtheworld.org
Email: inform@amritapuri.org

———————— *Fasting and Cleansing* ————————

First edition: January 2014

Copyright © 2014 by Mata Amritanandamayi Mission Trust,
Amritapuri, Kerala, India

Om karunamrita sagarayai namah

*Salutations to Her who is the ocean
of the nectar of compassion.*

**Sosanam bhavasindhosca,
jnapanam sarasampadah
Guroh padodakam samyak,
tasmai sri gurave namah**

*Salutations to the Guru, the water sanctified by the
touch of whose feet dries up the ocean of illusion
and reveals the true and only contentment.*

*I offer this book with all love and devotion
at the sacred Lotus Feet of my beloved
Satguru Sri Mata Amritanandamayi Devi.
May Her compassion and grace forever bless us.*

Lord Dhanvantari is regarded as the source of Ayurveda. Dhanvantari is depicted as Vishnu with four hands, holding medical herbs in one hand and a pot containing rejuvenating nectar of immortality called amrita in another.

Om namo bhagavate vasudevaya
danvantraye amrita kalasa hasthaya,
sarvamaya vinasanaya trilokya nathaya
sri maha vishnave namah

Salutations to Vasudeva, Lord of the universe, who has incarnated in the form of Dhanvantari, who holds the pot of ambrosia in his hands, who removes all disease, who is the Lord of the three worlds and who is none other than Lord Vishnu himself.

Contents

Sri Mata Amritanandamayi Devi

Through Her extraordinary acts of love and self-sacrifice, Mata Amritanandamayi, or Amma (Mother) as She is known, has endeared Herself to millions of people around the world. Tenderly caressing everyone who comes to Her, holding them close to Her heart in a loving embrace, Amma shares boundless love with all – regardless of their beliefs, who they are or why they have come to Her. In this simple yet powerful way, Amma is transforming the lives of countless people, helping their hearts to blossom, one embrace at a time. In the past 38 years, Amma has physically hugged more than 32 million people from all parts of the world.

Her tireless spirit of dedication to uplifting others has inspired a vast network of charitable activities through which people are discovering the sense of peace that comes from selflessly serving others.

Amma's teachings are universal. Whenever She is asked about her religion, She replies that Her religion is love. She does not ask anyone to believe in God or to change their faith, but only to inquire into their own real nature and to believe in themselves.

*Health and Consciousness
through Fasting and Cleansing*

Among the wide array of charitable projects that have been inspired by Amma are free homes for the poor, disaster relief work, an orphanage, free food, medicine and pensions for destitute women, sponsored weddings for the poor, free legal aid, prisoner's welfare programs, extensive health care programs that include multi-specialty hospitals and medical camps which offer free health care to the poor, and many schools, colleges and educational programs. For more information on Amma's charitable activities, please visit:

www.embracingtheworld.org
www.amritapuri.org
www.amma.org

Preface

The inspiration to write this book came from the book *Drugless, Sound Health Management (Auto Healing)* by Swami Vinayananda Giri, published by Mata Amritanandamayi Mission Trust, March 2011. His book contains a wealth of knowledge based on the principles of traditional Ayurveda, Naturopathy and Yoga. While his book expounds on Universal Truths, it was written primarily for an India-based audience. The goal of this book is to offer this ancient wisdom and knowledge to all people of all races and religious beliefs and of every country. With Swami's permission and blessing, this book comes to you as a completely revised, updated and expanded version of that original book.

The first section of this book addresses the foundational principles of Ayurveda and Naturopathy. The second section explores specific methods for creating and sustaining vibrant health while striving to attain the goals of life.

The human body is the most precious blessing from God. Thus, it needs to be properly honored and maintained. Honoring and maintaining the body is vital for sustaining perfect health and longevity. The human body is the most complicated of all bodies, which also means that it has the highest potential for malfunction. There is something else that only human beings possess— the intellect. Through the intellect, we can understand the body, how it functions, what leads to disease and what leads to perfect health. The goal of this book is to explain how to manage health without drugs or medicine. Health and Consciousness Through Fasting and Cleansing discusses how to live in harmony with natural laws, both physically and spiritually. By living in harmony and balance with Nature, perfect health can be achieved and maintained. Perfect health includes compassion, wisdom and mental equanimity (peace). Through the path of Ayurveda, Naturopathy and Yoga, this book will discuss how to create and sustain a healthy, continuous flow of *Prana* (Vital Universal Life Force) through the body for profound healing effects. Additionally, it will discuss how to determine what, when and how much food to eat, as well as the healing effects of *hatha yoga*, *pranayama* and fasting. It is my sincere prayer that this book serves as a valuable compendium of self-health knowledge. Through Amma's Divine Grace, may it benefit humankind.

Original foreword by Swami Vinayananda Giri from *Drugless Sound Health Management (Auto Healing)*

This book is about "Auto Healing." Auto Healing means that the human body has enormous, inherent powers to heal itself of disease by its own inner resources. These inner powers are "*Prana* (Universal Life Force), *Atma-Bala* (Strength or Power of the Soul) and *Manas Shakti* (mental power)." We have to provide the body with the right opportunity so that these inner powers can promote healing. This human body is not just a physical entity. It is the subtle and invisible pranic energy that actually sustains the body and directly controls all of the body's inner and outer activities. It is the manas, which is the subtlest energy in the body that motivates the prana. It is like a vehicle that is set into motion because petrol supplies it the required energy, and it is the driver who initiates the driving force. The body is like a vehicle, prana is like petrol, manas is like the driver and Atma is like the owner. To affect health, all these four factors, body (through dieting), mind (by positive attitude), prana (by right living) and Atma (by spiritual activity), have to be taken into consideration.

The modern medical system is slow to acknowledge the presence and activity of pranic energy in the body. Modern medicine is barely beginning to understand the role of mind in health and healing. Furthermore, they have ignored the omnipotent powers of Atma, which actually sustains the body and mind through prana.

Ayurveda, as taught by the rishis, emphasizes the importance of both prana and Atma in the healing process. Pranic healing, acupressure, acupuncture, marma chikitsa, naturopathy and reiki all directly deal with prana.

Ayurveda says "*swasthyatura parayanaha jeevitam ayuhu.*" This means that the secret of health is not about administering medicine to cause healing, but managing health in such a manner that no disease ever visits. The same thing is said by Hippocrates, the father of modern medicine – "Let food be your medicine and medicine be your food." This book deals with this aspect of health and healing. Health care in many countries has become prohibitively expensive. The modern doctors are more and more dependent upon exorbitantly expensive machines, expensive medicines and prohibitively expensive surgeries. All these put a heavy burden on the purse of the patients.

The modern healing system, being primarily symptomatic, aims only at removing the symptom while leaving the cause of the disease untouched. This, over a period of time, paves the way for chronic conditions. This is because the primary cause of the disease is still lying dormant in the body. The modern system of medicine, rather than curing chronic diseases, often focuses on administering palliative treatment. This often means the patient will have to live a long life filled with drugs and diseases. To put it in simple layman's language – "repeat the dose (of medicine) until the disease along with the patient dies!" This creates the potential of the onset of other associated diseases. For example, diabetes is said to be the mother of many other associated diseases pertaining to the kidneys, heart, skin, eyes, blood pressure, etc. There are also numerous side effects to modern drugs, creating additional maladies.

In contrast, the Auto Healing system directly deals with the cause of all diseases, whether acute or chronic, by advocating living as per God's natural laws. When the tenets of Auto Healing are followed scrupulously, it immensely strengthens the mind, which in turn invigorates the prana. This newly invigorated prana flows throughout the body harmoniously and initiates a free flow of pure blood reaching every cell. Thus, the pure blood supplies nutrients appropriately to all the body parts and flushes out the *Ama* (metabolic waste) while regenerating cells. This is how Auto Healing works without having to resort to medication.

It may look simple because it is simple. In nature, every thing is simple, meaning that when we respect the laws of the nature and abide by them, perfect health becomes our nature. Respecting and living in alignment with nature are abiding by divine law.

God has created this human body and is residing in the body as all-powerful "Atma." Then why should this body ever fall ill with so many diseases at all? Some diseases disfigure the body with no cure. The obvious answer is when we abuse the body through wrong living and wrong thinking, it becomes the victim of many varieties of diseases. Auto Healing will guide people to live life in accordance with God's divine laws. This is bound to bring health and happiness, peace and prosperity, success and security and, above all, compassion and wisdom.

Compassion and wisdom are the extra-special benefits of living as per God's divine laws through 'Auto Healing.'

May God and the great ones bless us all!

— Swami Vinayananda Giri

CHILDREN GO DIRECTLY TO THE SOURCE OF LOVE
AND DRINK TO YOUR HEART'S CONTENT
FROM THAT OCEAN.

AMMA

Part 1 – The foundations of creation

Chapter 1

Ayurveda and Naturopathy
– the way of Nature

*Everything in God's creation has a purpose and a
benefit, whatever it is. There is a use for everything,
whether it is a dog, a cat or a hen. No matter whether
it is an animal or a plant, there is a purpose behind its
creation. Even if human beings do not have any use for
something, other creatures do. The harmony of Nature
depends on all things that have been created. Take, for
example, the changes in weather patterns that have now
occurred. Because trees have been needlessly cut down,
we do not get the proper rainfall during the monsoon
season. Furthermore, the temperature has increased,
hasn't it? The trees are what purify the atmosphere,
absorbing all the impure air exhaled by human beings.*

– Amma (Awaken Children Vol.3, p.76)

Health and Consciousness
through Fasting and Cleansing

Ayurveda, the "science of life," is the ancient wisdom science of living in harmony with each other and our environment. It is a part of the spiritual tradition of *Sanatana Dharma*, or the Eternal Truth. Because Sanatana Dharma transcends all boundaries of caste, creed, nationality and religion, it is applicable to all people of all places and times. The knowledge of Ayurveda was given to us by the ancient *rishis* (seers). It expounds spiritual insights for living happy, healthful and peaceful lives, while seeking the ultimate goal of Self-realization. Ayurveda also incorporates the mystical science of yoga and *Vedanta* (the philosophy of non-dual or unified consciousness). The knowledge of Ayurveda is found in all of the four *Vedas*. The main Ayurveda text, the *Charaka Samhita*, describes the nature of the universe with all its manifestations and how to bring us into harmony with it. The deeper implications of Ayurveda are that it offers real freedom from disease as well as a path to immortality. Ayurveda's approach to health care aims to eliminate disease in such a way that it eventually leads to a spiritual awakening.

Ayurveda is the traditional natural healing system of India. The concept of Ayurveda is not just focused on medical treatment or diagnosis of a diseased condition;

it is a set of practical, simple guidelines for living a long and healthful life. Through these principles, we can bring our bodies and minds into perfect balance. Ayurveda has a theoretical basis, but it is also completely practical in nature. The word "Ayurveda" is composed of two words – *ayus* and *veda*. *Ayu* means "life" and Veda means "science." Together, the words mean "the knowledge of life." In Ayurveda, the process of ayu is considered as a combined experience of body, senses, psyche/mind and soul. Ayu represents all aspects of life, including death, dying and immortality.

The science of Ayurveda has developed over thousands of years. Today, it is at the forefront of body-mind-spirit medicines. Ayurveda has expanded far beyond its traditional base in India and is gaining recognition throughout the world. With its profoundly comprehensive understanding of life and consciousness, it is becoming the medicine of the present and future.

The main aims of Ayurveda are the prevention, treatment and cure of disease, as well as the promotion of health on four levels: physical, mental, emotional and spiritual.

Health and Consciousness through Fasting and Cleansing

Ayurveda teaches us how to create balance in order to attain perfect health. As we come to better understand the union of our body, mind and soul, we are able to extend our life span and enhance our wellbeing. The deeper purpose of this science, however, is to provide the opportunity for Self-realization, to know the true Self, *sat-chit-ananda* (Existence-Consciousness-Bliss). We must recognize that our bodies and minds are constantly changing in this world of duality. Our task is to discover the veiled part of us that is always there – the knower, the seer, the infinite, unchanging Source. With diligence, perseverance and patience, we can wake up from *Maya* (the dream/illusion) and become free of suffering. And as we awaken to our true Self, we create freedom in our body-mind-spirit. Ayurveda recognizes that we came to this earth to remember who we really are and to follow that dharma, to learn to take care of this physical existence while seeking *moksha* (liberation). When harmony of body, mind and spirit is established, we become free.

Naturopathy like Ayurveda is a philosophy that encompasses a completely holistic view of life, a model for living a full life. The word naturopathy is a Latin-Greek term that can be defined as 'being close to or benefiting from nature'. Traditional Naturopathy does not "diagnose" or "treat diseases," but rather recognizes that the majority of imbalances or degenerative health conditions are due to cumulative lifestyle effects, and that the underlying cause of what we call "disease" is simply improper eating, unhealthy habits, and environmental factors. These cause biological imbalances leading to a weakness of the bodies' natural immunity and subsequent deterioration and collapse in health.

Traditional Naturopathy promotes and teaches completely natural approaches to health such as fasting and detoxification, right diet, herbology, hydrotherapy, aromatherapy, exercise, rest, sunshine, and any other natural methods. Naturopathy uses non-invasive treatments and generally avoids drugs and surgery. Naturopathy focuses on prevention through naturally occurring substances, minimally invasive methods and the promotion of natural healing through cellular rejuvenation and strength.

Chapter 2

Sankhya philosophy

The Creator and the created are one and the same.
There is no separate Creator from the creation. The
Creator Him- or Herself has become the whole
of creation. There is no separation. So from this
point of view, it is like the waves in the ocean.
The waves are not different from the ocean. Even
though the waves have different shapes, lengths
and heights, they are not actually different from
the ocean. The ocean itself becomes the waves.

– Amma

To truly comprehend the way of nature and how the body and the world around us operates, we must look to the *Sankhya* Philosophy for answers. Due to intense sadhana (spiritual practices) and prayer, the Universal Truth or Ultimate Reality dawned within the minds of the rishis. The Sankhya philosophy, the foundation for Ayurveda and yoga, was given by the enlightened rishi Kapila. Sankhya has two meanings. The word *sankhya* translates as "to know truth" or "to understand truth."

Sankhya philosophy

San is truth and *khya* means to realize. Sankhya also means "number" or "to measure." The system gives an enumeration of twenty-four principles of the universe.

Sankhya philosophy: the 24 principles of creation (tattvas)

1.*Purusha* (Universal Consciousness) and *Prakriti* (Divine Manifestation or nature)
2. *Mahat* (Cosmic or Universal Intelligence) and *Buddhi* (differentiated individual intellect)
3. *Ahamkara* (Ego)From ahamkara the three *gunas* (universal qualities) manifest: *sattva, rajas, tamas*
4. *Manas* (mind)

Pancha jnanendriyas (Five sensory organs)

5. Hearing
6. Touch
7. Vision
8. Taste
9. Smell

Pancha karmendriyas (Five organs of action)

10. Speech
11. Grasping
12. Walking

13. Procreation
14. Elimination

Tanmatras (Objects of perception)

15. Sound (*Shabda*)
16. Touch (*Sparsha*)
17. Form (*Rupa*)
18. Taste (*Rasa*)
19. Smell (*Gandha*)

Mahabhutas (The elements)

20. Ether/Space (*Akasha*)
21. Air (*Vayu*)
22. Fire (*Agni*)
23. Water (*Apas*)
24. Earth (*Prithvi*)

The Sankhya philosophy enumerates the *tattvas* (twenty-four divine principles) that support the universal manifestation. The most important principles are those of purusha and prakriti. Everything emerges from prakriti and then is infused with purusha. Purusha (represented by *Shiva*, the Divine Masculine) and prakriti (represented by *Shakti,* the Divine Feminine) together form the fundamental basis of all manifestation. Prakriti and purusha are *anadi* (beginningless)

28

and *ananta* (infinite). Purusha is pure consciousness, all pervading and eternal. Prakriti is the doer and enjoyer. The true Self, *Atma*, when joined with the five great elements (*pancha mahabhutas*), becomes matter and thus assumes life. The pancha mahabhutas are the basic elements required for the formation of all the bodily tissues and sensory and motor organs, including the mind.

Purusha is the supreme Self, or Atman, that is beyond body consciousness. When the individual soul (*jiva*) returns to its original state (the supreme Self or Atman), the concepts of "I" and "mine" disappear. Purusha, or the Self, is beyond prakriti. It is subtle and omnipresent. It is beyond mind, intellect and the senses. It is the eternal seer, the witness.

Prakriti is the manifested, knowable source of all creation that can be experienced with attributes, name and form – that which is in time and space. Prakriti means "the first creation" or "to come into creation." It also means, "that which is primary, which precedes what is made." It comes from *pra* (before) and *kri* (to make or to do). Prakriti is the root cause of the universe and is called *pradhana*, or prime. All effects are founded on this principle. As such, it represents how we initially come into life before any fluctuations or modifications have taken place. Prakriti is the basis of existence. She is the Mother of the Universe. Prakriti represents the primordial will and its creative potential. It has form and attributes and can be named. It is the conscious will or choice to create. Divine will manifests through the activity of its own constituent gunas of mind: sattva, rajas and tamas. Amma has described the greater significance of the deep connections within creation this way: "*In order to feel real love and compassion, one must realize the oneness of the life force that sustains and is the substratum of the entire universe. Everything is pervaded by consciousness. It is that consciousness that sustains the world and all the creatures in it. To worship everything, seeing God in all, that is what religion advises.*"

Chapter 3

Mahat and buddhi

Purusha and Prakriti gave birth to *Mahat*, Divine Consciousness/Cosmic Intelligence. Mahat means "great" and applies to the whole of creation. Creation is a wondrous, mystical dance of the union of form and formlessness. Mahat is perfect. It is universal, the ideal creation, transcendental beyond time and space. Divine Consciousness comes down to the level of individual manifestation and becomes discrimination. Discrimination is the conscious awareness of truth and untruth, right and wrong, eternal and transient. Through the power of discrimination, the Divine Mind merges back into itself.

When mahat becomes individualized it is known as *buddhi*, the intellect with the power of thought and reason. Mahat joined with buddhi becomes a jiva, the individual consciousness. The jiva is the soul in union with the senses. It is housed in the body and is empowered by ego. It is associated with ignorance and karma. It is subject to pleasure and pain, to actions and their fruits, and constantly repeats the cycle of birth and death (reincarnation).

Health and Consciousness through Fasting and Cleansing

The intellect, or the buddhi, is the most important of all the manifestations of prakriti. The senses offer their objects to the intellect. The intellect is the instrument that is the medium between the sense organs and the Self. All of the concepts and projections that arise from sensation, reflection or consciousness are recorded and stored in the intellect before they become known to the Self. The intellect discriminates between purusha and prakriti, between the real and the unreal, between truth and untruth. Amma says, "*Train the mind using the weapons of discrimination and detachment in order to convince yourself that the body is non-eternal. What is the body after all, except a bag of excrement, flesh and blood? This is the thing that you dress with beautiful clothes and golden ornaments. Try to pierce through and see the real thing, which makes it beautiful and shining. That is the Supreme Consciousness.*"

Chapter 4

Ahamkara

From mahat and buddhi, *ahamkara* (ego) is formed. Ahamkara translates as the individual consciousness, the feeling that "I" exist. It is through the manifestation of ego that consciousness, veiled by *maya* (illusion), starts to take on false identities. It is this that creates the perception of limited individuality. The limited, individuated mind is born of ahamkara. It carries out the orders of the ego's will through the organs of action (*karmendriyas*). As an individual consciousness, the ego separates and divides things. It is the part of creation that is maya, acting as a veil over the supreme nature of reality. As the ego continues to divide, all things in the transient world come into manifestation. The intellect, the mind and the ego are like gatekeepers, and the five senses or organs of perception (*jnanendriyas*) are the gates. Ahamkara is the process of all division. It determines "this is this" and "that is that." It is from ahamkara that all diseases manifest. The wrong use of the karma and jnanendriyas creates an imbalance in our body, mind and soul. This wrong use leads to disease, death and destruction. It is the cause of war and poverty. We must learn the proper use of the indriyas and live in harmony with Mother Nature and humanity. Amma gives numerous examples to describe the nature of ahamkara. She says, "*The ego creates division. It can be compared to the walls that delineate the divisions of a house. If you demolish the walls, the house disappears and again you have only space. Remove the ego and you will again become space. The shell around the seed has to break before the tree can emerge. You have to get rid of the ego before you gain knowledge. When there is a curtain over the window, we cannot see the blue sky. If we remove the sense of 'I' from our mind, we will be able to see the light within us.*"

Chapter 5

Manas

*Children, when you sit for meditation, do not think
that you can still your mind immediately. At first,
you should relax all parts of your body. Loosen your
clothes if they are too tight. Make sure that the
spine is erect. Then close your eyes and concentrate
your mind on your breath. You should be aware
of your inhalation and exhalation. Normally we
breathe in and out without being aware of it, but
it should not be like that; we should become aware
of the process. Then the mind will be wakeful.*

— Amma

Ahamkara gives way to manas, which is the mind
bound by time, space, name and form. It operates
completely through the world of the senses. As such,
the mind is both an organ of sensation and of action.
The senses receive numerous impressions from the
external world. The mind then agrees with the senses,
and the impressions are perceived and formulated into
concepts. The mind thinks, the intellect determines,
and ego becomes conscious and projects itself back

onto the world. The gunas (universal qualities) and
tanmatras (objects of perception) are also manifestations of manas. Manas manifests from the sattvic and
rajasic properties of the ahamkara. It has the ability to
discriminate and create a peaceful, sattvic existence. It
is also necessary for action to occur. There is a profound
saying to demonstrate this point, "The mind makes a
horrible master but an excellent servant."

One really important aspect of creating balanced
health is a healthy mind. A healthy mind is developed
from loving discipline. According to the *Charaka Samhita*, we should exert mental and moral disciplines,
including:
• Respect God, teachers, saints and elderly people
• Be of help to others in times of difficulty
• Make firm decisions, be fearless, intelligent, brave
and forgiving
• Avoid negative, wicked and greedy people
• Avoid undesirable places, alcohol and drugs

Strict mental discipline and adherence to moral values
are vital to maintaining mental health. One of the key
concepts of Ayurveda demonstrates that abnormal
codes of conduct produce stress, and that errors or lack
of judgment are at the root of all stress. An improved

code of conduct prevents stress and can free the body
and mind from physical and mental disorders.

*We must always bear in mind that we are not going
to be free, but are free already. Every idea that we
are happy or unhappy is a tremendous delusion.*

– Swami Vivekananda

Chapter 6

The three gunas

Om iccha sakti jnana sakti kriya
sakti svarupinyai namah

I worship Her who is the form of the
powers of will, knowledge and action.

— Sri Lalita Sahasranama, verse 658

The three gunas, known as sattva, rajas and tamas, are the universal qualities of the fluctuations in the mind. They each manifest on a universal cosmic level and on an individual level, including in our own bodies and in all of nature. The three gunas are never separate; they support and intermingle as intimately as the flame, oil and wick of a lamp. They form the very substance of prakriti. All objects are composed of the three gunas, which act on one another. In the *Chandogya Upanishad* it is said that the sound *AUM* is the totality of the three gunas. *A* is the state of sattva, and is the waking state or the subjective consciousness. It is represented by Brahma, the Creator. *U* is rajas and the dream state. It is represented by Vishnu, the Preserver. *M* is

tamas, the yogic sleep state of undifferentiated awareness, represented by Shiva, the Destroyer or the great
Transformer.

The gunas are the primary original qualities or states
of mind. These vibrational frequencies and attitudes
are found in the mind as well as in all of creation. The
three qualities of the mind are directly connected with
the doshas. It is the gunas that attach the consciousness
to the physical body. The mental nature of a person
can be categorized according to these gunas. The three
gunas are *sattva* (pure or essence), *rajas* (movement)
and *tamas* (inertia). The three gunas are found in all of
nature as well as in the mind. Ayurveda offers a clear
description of people on the basis of their psychological constitution (*manas prakriti*). All individuals have
a combination of the three, wherein the predominant
guna determines an individual's mental nature.

When in balance, the three gunas maintain a
healthy state of mind and, to some extent, of body as
well. The three gunas are the very fabric of creation as
they permeate through all living and non-living, tan-
gible and intangible things. An object's predominant
guna determines the vibrations it emits and its behavior. Disturbances to the harmony of the gunas result in

different types of mental disorders. The development of a sattvic mind is goal of yoga and Ayurveda.

The three gunas manifest in our body, mind and consciousness. As they are subtler than the doshas, disturbances in the gunas create disturbances in the gross body. The gunas make up our mental disposition and spiritual inclinations. Everyone has some proportion of sattva, rajas and tamas. The key is to keep them balanced and in harmony with each other and with the manas prakriti. The goal of yoga is to balance and control tamas, rajas and sattva within one's consciousness.

Sattva

Often considered to be the pure state of mind or consciousness, sattva is a clear, light, innocent and undisturbed inner state of being. Content and divine in nature, sattva is the union of the heart and mind. It is virtuous, patient and compassionate – the mind in its natural state of pure being.

A sattvic mind reflects clarity of perception and peace of mind. One endowed with a sattvic nature is free from suffering and is a beacon of light for the world. Sattvic types are always engaged in good actions and work toward the betterment of humanity. Sattva is the pure manifestation of the cosmic and individual mind. Sattva is pure light, dharma, consciousness, creativity and the power of observation. Sattva gives the power of discrimination, knowledge and the ability to know the truth. The pure state of sattva manifests as peace, harmony, contentment, compassion, unconditional love, selflessness, devotion and faith. Sattva is equilibrium. When sattva prevails, there is peace and tranquility. When sattva is predominant, it overpowers rajas and tamas.

Rajas

Rajas is the nature of movement and action. It has the power of observation. Rajas is the active force that moves sattva into action. With rajas present, the pure mind is disturbed, agitated and active. With the mind's gaze looking outward, we start desiring; thus, rajas is the essence of desire. The most active of the gunas, rajas characterizes motion and stimulation. All desires and aspirations are a result of rajas. It influences all endeavors, including the logical, rational, thinking mind. It creates indecisiveness, unreliability, hyperactivity and anxiety. Rajas generates lust and greed for money, material luxuries and comfort. When one has desire, attachment follows. These attachments are the cause of all suffering. Rajas is self-serving and considers its own interests first, at any cost. When desires are not fulfilled, more suffering results.

Rajas, when balanced with sattva, manifests love and compassion. When disturbed it brings anger, rage, hostility and disease. Rajas is the manifestation of ego or individualization. The five organs of action (mouth, hands, feet, reproductive organs and eliminatory organs) come from rajas. The mind is also the active principle of rajas.

Rajas is the active, vital, ever-changing, moveable principle. Rajas provides the shakti (energy) for creation to be perceived. We find rajas in the changeability of the mind and thoughts that shift from one end of the spectrum to another without rest. Activity that is expressed as likes and dislikes, love and hatred, attraction and repulsion, is rajas. It is the energy that observes and perceives through the intellect. Without rajas, sattva is unmoveable. Rajas is necessary for creation. Through rajas one experiences the senses, the world and individuality. It is the energy that makes one desirous and seek sense pleasure. Rajas is also the energy that gives us the ability to discriminate between the eternal and non-eternal. When rajas becomes dominant, it overpowers sattva and tamas. When in harmony, it destroys tamas and activates sattva.

The three gunas

Tamas

Tamas is the nature of destruction, dissolution and darkness. Tamas is the inability to perceive light or consciousness. Excess tamas is inertia. Heaviness and resistance characterize Tamas. Delusion, laziness, apathy and drowsiness are caused by it. Sedative in nature, tamas causes pain and suffering and leads to depression.

Tamas manifests as blocked emotions. Tamas is the nature of destruction, degeneration and death. It is unfulfilled desire sup- pressed in the recesses of the subconscious mind. The presence of tamas creates vindictiveness, violence, hatred, criminality and psychopathic behavior. Its nature is animalistic, delusional, self- serving, materialistic and demonic. Because tamas contains all the doshas, it rules over the earth and the five elements.

Rajas is necessary for creation. Through rajas one experiences the senses, the world and individuality. It is the energy that makes one desirous and seek sense pleasure. Rajas is also the shakti that gives us the ability to discriminate between the eternal and non-eternal. When rajas is dominant, it overpowers sattva and tamas. When in harmony, it destroys tamas and activates sattva.

Chapter 7

The tanmatras

The gunas manifest as *tanmatra*s (the five sensory perceptions), jnanendriyas (the five sense organs), karmendriyas (the five organs of action), and *pancha mahabhutas* (the five elements). *Sattvaguna* is responsible for the five sense organs, the five motor organs and mind/consciousness. *Tamasguna* is responsible for the five sensory perceptions and the five elements. *Rajasguna* connects sattvaguna and tamasguna.

The tanmatras or senses are manifest in all life forms in all of creation. The tanmatras and indriyas emerge out of un-manifest matter, prakriti. These are the subtle forms of the five elements in their vibrational state of being. The tanmatras are *shabda* (sound), *sparsha* (touch), *rupa* (form or sight), *rasa* (taste) and *gandha* (smell). These subtleties are responsible for our ability to sense and objectify the external world. Shabda relates to the ether element, sparsha to air, rupa to fire, rasa to water and gandha to earth.

The tanmatras directly relate to the mahabhutas. Everything in this entire universe consists of different combinations of these five elements: ether, air, fire, water and earth. They represent the ether, gaseous, radiant or light, liquid and solid forms that make up the physical universe, including our bodies. Each element corresponds and relates to one of the tanmatras in a dynamic, creative way. Ether corresponds to sound/hearing; air to touch; fire to sight; water to taste; and earth to smell.

The tanmatras and the five elements are also directly related to the jnanendriyas and karmendriyas, through which they express themselves. The five sense organs are ear, skin, eye, tongue and nose. The ear relates to shabda, sound and the ether element; skin to sparsha, touch and the air element; eyes to rupa, sight and the fire element; tongue to rasa, taste and the water element; and nose to gandha, smell and the earth element. The five organs of action also relate to the five sense organs and the five elements. They are the mouth, hands, feet, urinogenital/ reproductive organs and anus. The mouth corresponds to the ether element and sound (shabda). The hands relate to the air element (sparsha) and touch. The feet relate to the fire element (rupa) and sight. The urogenital/reproductive organs relate to taste and the water element (rasa), and the anus relates to smell and the earth element (gandha).

All of these sense organs are responsible for our relative experiences and bring consciousness into form. Each of the organs, elements, tanmatras and sense organs has unique characteristics that make up the temporal world.

Chapter 8

The five elements

Treat the Earth well. It was not given to you
by your parents; it was loaned to you by your
children. We do not inherit the Earth from our
ancestors; we borrow it from our children.

— Native American Proverb

Consciousness takes form as the five great elements through which we know creation. From these, all of the many objects of the external world are composed. The mahabhutas are experienced in the subtle (non-physical) realm. From and within space/ether emanates air (thinness, lightness, airiness), then fire (energy), then water (flow, fluidity), then earth (solidity, form).

In daily life, it is helpful to be aware of the elements and what a vital part they play in sustaining creation. Awareness leads us to gratitude, which in turn leads us to love and patience. When we live a life of gratitude we are at peace with ourselves and nature. Amma gives great importance to the five elements and the vital role that they play. Amma says, "*There is no inert matter in the creation of God. Without earth, we cannot live. Earth is the substratum of our life. So we are taught by the Eternal Truth (Sanatana Dharma) to worship Mother Earth. By worshipping Mother Earth, we can avoid ecological degradation. Similarly, water is worshipped as God because we cannot live without water. Also, agni (fire) is worshipped. We need heat to live. Both extremes of heat and cold would make it impossible to live. So we need a right balance of all the natural resources. The same is true of air. This is why all the five great elements are worshipped in Hinduism. In Sanatana Dharma we are taught to visualize unity in diversity."*

The five elements form the basis of all things that are a part of creation. To balance them in a way that is unique for every human is the basic principle of Ayurveda.

Ether or Space

Space is where we live, and this is the place where everything happens; it is the container of creation. It can also be called the stage where *lila* (the divine play) unfolds. The cells of our bodies also contain space. Ether is the subtlest of all the elements. Ether manifests as pure ideas and inspiration, and allows the connectivity and exchange between all things. It manifests as self-expression, holding space for creation to birth itself.

It is expansive, subtle, light, clear, infinite and eternal. Ether comes from consciousness and the mind, and later returns to consciousness. When ether moves from its original, un-manifest state it becomes air.

Air

Air is transparent and lofty, and causes activity within space. The biological functions that originate from sensations are considered to be functions of air. Likewise, the movements of thought and desire, which are functions of the mind, are also considered to be a function of air. Air is light, mobile, clear, dry, rough, and inconsistent and like the changing wind. Air is the subtle movement responsible for directional force; it is in constant flux, ever changing. Air is the power of propulsion and, when it moves fast enough, causes friction and creates light or fire.

Fire

Movements cause friction and thereby produce heat, which we call fire, the third element. This process changes matter from one state to another. Fire assists in the functions of the body, e.g., digestion and absorption. Fire has the qualities of being hot, sharp, liquid or fluid, penetrating, light, luminous, ascending and dispersing. The fire element also gives perception. Fire radiates heat and gives direction (internal and external) through sight and insight. When fire condenses, it becomes water.

Water

Water represents the liquid state and is necessary for the survival of all living beings. Our body is composed primarily of water. Bodily fluids, including blood, saliva and hormones, help our body to transport energy and remove waste products. Water is fluid, heavy, wet, lubricating, cooling, softening, cohesive and stable. It is part of the impulse that nurtures and gives birth to life and is related to the reproductive organs and the conception process. Water is also womb-like in its nurturing qualities; it gives birth to new creative ideas and processes. When water coagulates, it becomes earth.

Earth

Earth represents the solid state. The solid and stable structures of the human body are created from the earth element. It feeds and provides sustenance for all living things, and therefore creates a sense of permanence and security. Earth has the qualities of being thick, dense, hard, solid, heavy and stable.

The five elements

Each element contains one-tenth of the previous element. Ether is the self-sustaining substratum in which creation takes place. Ether is in air. Air and ether are in fire. Fire, air and ether are in water. And all of the elements exist in earth.

The *doshas* (bodily constitutions) arise from the five elements. The concept of the doshas was evolved by the rishis of Ayurveda to differentiate between sentient and non-sentient beings. The *sarira* (human body) is made up of the pancha mahabhutas. Life blossoms only when the Atma, indriyas and manas unify within the human frame. Doshas are the biological units of the living body, and are responsible for all its functions.

There are three doshas – *vata*, *pitta* and *kapha* – each of which is made of a combination of the mahabhutas. *Vayu* (wind) and *akash* (space) form vata, agni forms pitta, and *jala* (water) and *prithvi* (earth) form kapha dosha.

The word dosha is derived from the word *dusa,* which means, "to vitiate." In the balanced state of equilibrium the doshas support and nourish the body, and when vitiated they produce disease.

The principles of Sankhya philosophy are the basis and sub- stratum of Ayurveda. The path of Ayurveda is a means of awakening. When awareness of the Self, awakens in our consciousness, we are eternally free. The scriptures say that the whole universe dwells inside the Self. All the principles of Sankhya are part and parcel of that one Self. As we incorporate the principles of Ayurveda into our lives, may we awaken fully on the journey from darkness to light, from death to immortality.

> *A human being is part of the whole,*
> *called by us Universe.*
>
> – Albert Einstein

Chapter 9

The doshas and gunas

The doshas

The most fundamental and characteristic principle of Ayurveda is that of *tridosha,* or the three humors. All matter is composed of the five elements (*pancha mahabhutas*) that exhibit the proper- ties of earth (*prithvi*), water (*jala*), fire (*tejas*), wind (*vayu*) and space (*akasha*). All of creation is a dance or a play of these five elements. The structural aspect of our body is made up of these five elements, but the functional aspect of the body is governed by three doshas. Ether and air constitute vata; fire, pitta; and water and earth, kapha. They govern psychobiological changes in the body and physio-pathological changes. Vata, pitta and kapha are present in every cell, tissue and organ.

Doshas are to be seen as all-pervasive, subtle manifestations. Vata regulates movement and governs the nervous system. Pitta is the principle of biotrans-formation and governs the metabolic processes in the body. Kapha is the principle of cohesion and functions through the body fluids. In each individual, the three doshas manifest in different combinations and thereby determine the physiologic constitution (prakriti) of an individual. Vata, pitta and kapha manifest differently in each human being according to the predominance of their gunas.

The word dosha actually means, "vitiated" or "out of balance." Imbalances occur due to factors such as improper diet, seasonal changes, physical or mental stress, etc. Imbalances occur to protect the body from physiological harm. In harmonious conditions, the doshas sustain a balance within us. The doshas are responsible for biological, psychological and physio-pathological processes in our body, mind and consciousness. They can maintain homeostasis or wreak havoc in our lives when they are disturbed. Each individual in creation is a unique blend of the three doshas. When the tridoshas are balanced, the individual experiences health on all levels, mental, physical and spiritual.

When the following characteristics are in place, the doshas are said to be in balance, and a harmonious state of health is achieved.
• Happiness – a sense of wellbeing
• Emotions – evenly balanced emotional states

• Mental Functions – good memory, comprehension, intelligence and reasoning ability
• Senses – proper functioning of eyes, ears, nose, taste and touch
• Energy – abundant mental and physical energy
• Digestion – easy digestion of food and drink• Elimination – normal elimination of wastes: sweat, urine, feces and others
• Physical Body – healthy bodily tissues, organs and systems.

There are generally two types of imbalances – natural and unnatural. Natural imbalances are due to time and age. These natural imbalances can be rectified through lifestyle adjustments. Unnatural imbalances of the doshas can be caused by inappropriate diet or lifestyle, physical, mental or emotional trauma, viruses, parasites, etc. While some of these factors are beyond our control, the way we live, the foods we eat and our actions are within our control. By following the correct lifestyle regime for our personal dosha, we can minimize unnatural disturbances.

The gunas

The doshas are composed of the five elements. Ojas, tejas and prana are the very subtle forms of the doshas. These three are the positive, life-giving aspects of the doshas. Prana is our vital life force and is the healing energy of vata. Tejas is our inner light and is the healing energy of pitta. Ojas is the ultimate energy reserve of the body that manifests from kapha. In Ayurveda, one wants to reduce excess in the doshas to prevent disease, while developing more prana, tejas and ojas for good health. A person with strong, healthy prana has vitality, breath, circulation, movement and adaptability. Someone endowed with good tejas has radiance, luster in the eyes, clarity, insight, courage, compassion and fearlessness. A person with strong ojas has strong immunity, endurance, calmness and contentment. Like the doshas, it is necessary that the gunas be in alignment with each other and within our consciousness, giving us physical, psychological and spiritual stamina.

Prana, tejas and ojas are the divine manifestations of the three doshas. According to Ayurveda, when the doshas are too high or too low, they cause disease. But prana, tejas and ojas, unlike the doshas, promote health, creativity and wellbeing and provide support for deeper sadhana. Prana, tejas and ojas do not cause disease. They are the radiant manifestations in our life. We only have disease if they are imbalanced or lacking. As with all things in creation, conditions of excess and deficiency can arise when prana, tejas and ojas are out of balance.

Ojas

The most crucial factor in wellness is ojas. Ojas is the essential root power, our basic energy. It is the accumulated vital reserve, the basis of physical and mental energy. Ojas is the internalized essence of digested food, water, air, impressions and thoughts. On an inner level it is responsible for nourishing and developing all higher facilities. Ojas is our core vitality. It is the basic capacity of the immune system to defend us against external pathogens. Ojas provides endurance, resistance and strength to ward off disease. It affords not only physical immunity, but emotional and mental immunity as well. It is a superfine substance that gives strength to the bodily tissues, organs and processes. Ojas is the motherly qualities of nurturance and love. Without ojas we become lifeless. Ojas is the pure vibration of love and compassion in the heart. When one is filled with love, the gross and subtle immune system is very strong and disease cannot penetrate into the body. Ojas is the product of pure thoughts and actions as well as the intake of pure foods and impressions. It gives us mental strength, contentment, purity, patience, calmness, adaptability and excellent mental faculties. Ojas is increased and maintained through proper diet (sattvic, vegetarian or vegan diet), tonic herbs, sensory control (including celibacy or proper use of sexual energy) and Bhakti Yoga (including seva).

Tejas

Tejas is our inner light and the subtle energy of the fire element, pitta. It is the radiant mental vitality through which we digest air, impressions and thoughts. On an inner level, it opens up higher perceptual abilities. Tejas is the fire of the intellect, knowledge and reason. It gives the power of proper discrimination such as knowing the eternal from the non-eternal and right from wrong. Tejas is the power of sadhana or spiritual practices such as self- discipline, scriptural study and mantra japa. Tejas is necessary for *Jnana Yoga*, the yoga of knowledge. It bestows clarity of mind and speech as well as courage and faith. It gives the power to know the Self and the endurance to persist on the path toward the One. Practices like *atma-vicharya* (Self-inquiry) increase the intensity of tejas within the mind and heart.

Like ojas, tejas is a vital part of our immunity. Tejas is the immune system's ability to burn and destroy toxins. When activated, it generates fever to destroy pathogens that assault the body. Tejas is our ability to attack and overcome acute diseases, which are generally infectious in nature. As fire, it is the power of digestion and the transformation of our food, thoughts, emotions and actions. Someone with strong tejas will have bright, penetrating eyes, lustrous skin and an attractive personality.

Tejas can be increased and maintained by performing tapas (purification through the heat or spiritual practices), such as controlling the tongue (fasting and observing silence). It is often said that if we cannot control the tongue we will never be able to control the mind. Chanting of mantras is an excellent way to harness the pure quality of the tongue and the mind. Studying scriptures is also very beneficial. One must do spiritual practices under the guidance of a competent guide so as to protect tejas from becoming too high.

If tejas becomes too high, it can deplete ojas and harm the nervous system.

Prana

Prana is our vital life force and the subtle energy of the air element, vata. As the divine force and guiding intelligence behind all psychophysical functions, it is responsible for the coordination of the breath, senses and mind. On an inner level, it awakens and balances all higher states of consciousness. Prana governs all aspects of our life, physical and spiritual. Prana is our ability of coordination and speech. Prana is the essence of sound and governs all mantras. It is the breath that gives life; it literally breathes life into all of creation. It is our creative impulse and desire for evolution. Prana is the vitalized activation of the immune system's natural functions to project and develop our life force. It manifests when we are fighting off chronic diseases. It is the adaptability of the immune system and sustains all long-term healing processes. With sufficient prana, tejas and ojas, no disease can harm us.

Prana is increased through practices like meditation, pranayama, hatha yoga and the chanting of mantras, especially AUM. Prana is the unifying factor between ojas and tejas. Once ojas is present, tejas is born. Prana develops from the union of ojas and tejas. Ojas and tejas could not sustain themselves without prana.

Chapter 10

The dhatus

There are seven *dhatus*, or layers of tissue, in the human body. The word dhatu literally translates "to hold together," "to firm" or "to construct." Dhatus are the layers of bodily tissue that support and hold the body together, giving it form. The nutrients we receive from our digested food create the dhatus. Each tissue is governed by one of the three elements, and each dhatu is developed from the preceding tissue layer, beginning with *rasa* (plasma). If the plasma is not healthy, then all the other layers are affected. Each dhatu produces a secondary tissue known as its *upadhatu*, as well as a type of *mala* (waste material).

Dhatus are the sites in the body where diseases manifest. Each dhatu can be in excess, deficient or balanced in relation to the rest of the body. When one dhatu is diseased or impaired it affects the next dhatu and subsequently the next, as each receives its nutrients from the preceding one.

The seven dhatus in order of production are *rasa* (plasma), *rakta* (blood), *mamsa* (muscle), *meda* (fat), *asthi* (bone), *majja* (marrow and nerves), and *shukra/artava* (male/female reproductive fluid). Each dhatu is formed from the previous dhatu. Rasa becomes rakta, rakta becomes mamsa, mamsa becomes meda, meda becomes asthi, asthi becomes majja, and majja becomes shukra and artava. The formation of ojas is the final product of the nutritional process of the dhatus.

The seven dhatus

1. *Rasa dhatu* (plasma tissue). Rasa derives from digested food, and then nourishes each and every tissue and cell of the body; it is analogous to plasma. The upadhatus for rasa are breast milk and menstrual blood. The mala of rasa dhatu is phlegm.

2. *Rakta dhatu* (blood tissue). Rakta is viewed as the basis of life and is analogous to the circulating blood cells. It nourishes the body tissues and provides physical strength and color to the body. The upadhatus for rakta are the blood vessels, skin and tendons. The mala of rakta dhatu is bile.

3. *Mamsa dhatu* (muscle tissue). Mamsa is muscle tissue, and its main function is to provide physical strength and support for the meda dhatu. The upadhatus for mamsa are the ligaments and skin. The mala of mamsa dhatu is the waste materials of the outer bodily cavities like the ears and nose, for example earwax and nasal crust.

4. *Meda dhatu* (fat tissue). Meda consists of adipose (fat) tissue providing support to asthi dhatu. Meda lubricates the body. The upadhatu for meda is omentum, the peritoneal fat of the abdomen. The mala for meda dhatu is sweat.

5. *Asthi dhatu* (bone tissue). Asthi is comprised of bone tissue, including cartilage. Its main function is to give support to the majja and mamsa dhatus. The upadhatu of asthi is the teeth. The mala for asthi dhatu is the nails and hair.

6. *Majja dhatu* (marrow and nerve tissue). Majja denotes the bone marrow tissue, nervous system and brain. Its main function is to lubricate the body. It is a very soft, jelly-like substance that fills the bone cavity. The upadhatu for majja is the sclerotic fluid in the eyes. The mala of majja dhatu is the tears and other secretions of the eyes.

7. *Shukra and artava dhatu* (semen and reproductive tissue). The main purpose of the reproductive tissue is to aid in reproduction and to strengthen the body. The upadhatu for shukra and artava dhatus is ojas. The mala for shukra and artava dhatus is smegma, the waste secreted from the genitals.

Chapter 11

The malas

Mala is our body waste. The word *mala* means "bad" or "tainted." The three malas are the three types of waste materials in the body: feces, urine and sweat. Just like the organs and dhatus, the malas can have four types of imbalances: excess, deficiency, damage and increase/decrease.

Feces

An excess or build up of feces (*purisha*) can cause abdominal pain, abdominal cramping, constipation, heaviness and painful excretion. Results of deficiency include gas, dehydration of the intestines, abdominal distention, as well as lower back pain, palpitations, generalized body pain and prolapse of the colon. Deficiency is usually due to dryness caused by high vata. Feces can be damaged by excessive or wrong use of colonics or purgatives, eating the wrong foods for your dosha, wrong food-combining, excess movement or travel, stimulants, drugs, antibiotics, parasites and wrong use of sex. Feces can be increased with the use of laxatives like triphala and chitrak, as well as bran, whole grains, root vegetables and dark, leafy greens. Feces can be decreased by fasting, the use of purgatives and consuming light food or fruit juice.

Urine

Urine (*mutra*) in excess can cause pain, cramping or pressure in the bladder, frequent urination, or the feeling of having to urinate again immediately after urinating. When urine is deficient there may be difficulty when urinating, scanty urination, discoloration, blood in the urine and thirst. The urinary system is damaged by excessive use of diuretic herbs, drugs, food, alcohol and sex, as well as emotional disturbances like sudden shock or trauma to the body. Urine is increased by the intake of liquids and is decreased by fasting from liquids or by strong heat such as a sauna or sweat lodge.

Sweat

An excess of sweat (*svedha dhatu*) causes profuse perspiration, bad body odor and skin eruptions like eczema, psoriasis, boils and fungal invasions. When sweat is deficient, there will be stiffness and dryness of the hair on the skin, dry or wrinkled skin, dandruff and other surface deficiencies. Svedha is damaged by

66

excessive use of diuretics, saunas, sweat lodges, hot tubs, exercise (according to body type) and dry foods. It can also be damaged by a lack of salt in one's diet. Extreme or inadequate exercising (according to one's dosha) will also damage sweat production. Sweat can be increased by drinking sour fruit juice with salt and by exposure to heat like saunas, hot tubs and sweat lodges. It is decreased by exposure to cold and a decrease in water intake.

Chapter 12

Ama

Ama is a concept unique to Ayurveda. It is an essential causative factor of disease and the disease process. Ama begins with improperly digested or processed toxic particles that clog the body's physical channels. These channels include the intestines, lymphatic system, arteries and veins, capillaries and genitourinary tract. Ama accumulates wherever there is a weakness in the body and results in disease. There are five main causes of ama.

Causes of ama

1. *Agni-Mandya* – Low digestive fire

Digestive fire is a vital component of the complete and proper digestion of food. When digestive fire is low, food is not properly digested and toxins are formed. Absorption becomes sluggish and the poorly digested food and/or toxins are retained in the intestines. This retention causes the toxins to ferment and putrefy in the intestines. The ama remains unabsorbed in the intestines. Incomplete digestion is the root cause of most diseases.

2. *Dhatu-Agni-Mandya* – Low tissue fire

Dhatu-agni (dhatvagni) plays an important role in the process of forming tissues from nutrient substances. When the power of the dhatvagni of a particular tissue is diminished, either in the liver or in a channel, the nourishment and construction of that tissue is incomplete and ama is produced. When toxins are present in the tissues, it is called *samadhatu,* or tissues containing ama. This type of pathology is seen in most diseases. In diabetes, fat (meda dhatu) and muscle (mamsa dhatu) tissues are formed as "sama tissues" because of the diminished agni of the fat and muscle tissues. This disturbs the normal functioning activities of these tissues. In cases of obesity, a similar type of fat tissue is produced due to weak meda dhatu agni, or fire of fat tissue.

3. *Mala Sanchaya* – Accumulated waste products

Agni transforms food substances into body tissues. It first produces a nutritious substance, which is then converted into tissues in the second phase of digestion. This process, referred to as secondary or tissue digestion, is the anabolic activity of tissue fire. Different tissues are produced as a result of tissue fire's action on nutrient food substances. The tissues produced are utilized for the release of energy required for every bodily activity. During this process, the tissue substances are again digested, transformed and utilized for the release of heat and energy by the tissue fire. This describes the catabolic process. During this activity of tissue disintegration, minute, subtle waste products called *kleda* are formed. Small amounts of kleda are essential for the body; the excess is excreted. If this excretion is defective or deficient, kleda accumulates in the body and results in the formation of the toxic substance ama.

4. *Dosha Sammurcchana* – Interaction between vitiated doshas

Every dosha has unique qualities that are antagonistic to the qualities of other doshas. For example, the dry and light qualities of vata are antagonistic to the oily and heavy qualities of kapha. Likewise, the hot quality of pitta is antagonistic to the cold quality of kapha and vata. When two or three doshas become severely vitiated and combine, specific reactions between them occur. These conditions produce opposite qualities:

instead of nullifying each other, they interact and produce ama.

5. *Krimi Visha* – Bacterial toxins

When pathogenic organisms cause an infection, they release a toxic substance. Pathogenic organisms can include molds, fungus, yeast, worms, bacteria and various parasites.

Signs and symptoms of ama

• Obstruction can occur in any of the channels (srotas). The most commonly observed obstructions are in the liver, urinary tract, fallopian tubes, blood vessels, and the gastrointestinal and respiratory tracts.
• Weakness or deficiency in any part or organ of the body. Obstruction of the movement of vata: Ama causes disturbance in the action of the musculature of the part or organ and in the conduction of nerve impulses. Ultimately, the activity of the affected part diminishes or stops altogether.
• Heaviness and lethargy
• The tongue will be coated with a whitish, thick or greasy film, especially upon rising in the morning.
• Metabolic and digestive disturbances such as bloating, gas, constipation, diarrhea, sticky stool, sinking

stool, mucous or blood in the stool, fever, turbid urine, skin blemishes and foul- smelling stool, breath, sweat, urine and phlegm.

• One may lack mental clarity and energy and feel weary or unenthusiastic. One may even experience depression.

Modern symptoms of ama

High triglycerides, atherosclerosis, adult onset diabetes, high blood sugar levels, depression, rheumatoid factor, overgrowth of H. pylori bacteria, leukocytosis or leukocytopenia (deficient or excess white blood cells), excess antibodies, candida albicans in the gut and uterus, blood urea, gout, excess platelets, high IgE levels from allergic reactions, excess red blood cells, gallstones as a sign of excess bile, kidney stones as a sign of unmetabolized calcium and oxalates, high liver enzymes, glaucoma, bacterial infection, fever, tumors

Effects of ama

When ama comes in contact with the doshas, dhatus or waste products, it produces sama dosha, sama dhatus and sama mala. Ayurveda describes symptoms of these stages – sama (with ama) and *nirama* (without ama) – in the doshas, dhatus and malas for all diseases.

The underlying cause of any disease is an imbalance in one or all of the doshas. For successful treatment of a particular disease, the Ayurvedic Practitioner must determine whether the imbalanced dosha is sama or nirama.

Chapter 13

Agni

Agni is the transformative principle of fire. It is the source of light and love in the universe. Without light and love, we have no life force (prana). Without love, life is empty and meaningless. On the subtle level agni is tejas, the illuminating aspect of consciousness that governs our mental processes. It generates new ideas and inspiration, as well as the energy to manifest them. Each dosha, each dhatu, each kosha, each organ and each part of nature has its own agni. As the fire aspect of the five great elements (pancha mahabhutas), it exists in our bodies as the pitta dosha. Agni is the fire inside our body.

Agni encompasses all of the changes in the body and mind, from the dense to the subtle. These changes include the digestion and absorption of food, cellular transformations, assimilation of sensory perceptions, and mental and emotional experiences. The process of agni covers the whole sequence of chemical interactions and changes in the body and mind. It governs overall body metabolism.

Agni

Of the forty agnis existing in the human body, the primary are *jatharagni* (the digestive fire of the stomach), *dhatvagnis* (the seven dhatu agnis), and the five *bhutagnis* (the liver enzymes which process the components of food into elements of bodily tissue). There are also agnis for each of the srotas (channels). Without agni, the dhatus do not receive nourishment and disease manifests.

The most important agni is the jatharagni, the gastric or digestive fire responsible for digesting food. This agni correlates hydrochloric acid in the stomach and the digestive enzymes and juices secreted into the stomach, duodenum and the small intestine. Jatharagni is the main agni responsible for the digestion and the absorption of nutrients from food.

Balanced agni plays a vital role in maintaining optimum health, as it is necessary to destroy ama. As agni exists in every tissue and cell in the body, it is a necessary component in maintaining nutrition and the autoimmune mechanism. By destroying *krumi* (micro-organisms, foreign bacteria and toxins in the stomach and the intestines), agni helps to maintain health and interrupt the disease process.

Health and Consciousness
through Fasting and Cleansing

Agni protects us from both external as well as internal disorders. A disturbance or weakness of agni implies that the basic balance of the doshas has been disturbed. Disturbed or weakened metabolism, compromised immunity and lowered immune resistance are all results of impaired agni. When agni is weakened food will not be digested properly. It will not activate the chain of nutritional formation of the seven dhatus in a proper way. Instead of creating ojas, ama will be created and will accumulate in the body, clogging body channels and manifesting disease. Agni's functioning depends on many factors, including food, clothing and shelter. It also depends on the five senses: what we see, hear, smell, taste and touch. Negative or disturbing input may contribute to ill health. Positive and loving sensory input supports wellness.

Part 2 – The foundations of health

Chapter 14

The path to health

*To care for the body is a duty; otherwise
the mind will not be strong and clear.*

– Buddha

*If one way be better than another, that,
you may be sure, is nature's way.*

– Aristotle

*It is now the urgent duty of all human beings to
please nature by performing selfless actions endowed
with mutual love, faith and sincerity. When this is
done, nature will bless you back with abundance.*

– Amma

The very first thing we have to understand is that all of
our illnesses, whether acute or chronic, are the direct
result of imbalanced Agni, accumulation of Ama and

faulty Mala. There is an aphorism in Ayurveda that says, "*Mandaagnou sakala rogo moolam,*" meaning weak digestion is the root cause of all diseases. Other causes such as viral attacks, hormonal disturbances and organ failure are only secondary or symptomatic. When the process of digestion is disturbed the body becomes vulnerable to attacks due to a compromised immune system. This affects the superfine balance of the entire metabolic process. This imbalance is the direct cause of disease.

The *Kashyapa Samhita* declares, "*Aarogyam Annadheenam.*" This statement means that the state of our health and our happiness is dependent upon the kind of food we eat. Additionally, Ayurveda has a very enlightening definition of health and healing: "*Swasthyatura parayanaha jeevitam ayuhu.*" This means healing is not all about administering medicines to cure diseases, but instead ensuring that no disease ever manifests in the first place. This whole book is dedicated to this particular aspect of Ayurveda, the prevention of disease.

It is an interesting paradox, that most people, especially physicians, fail to understand is that of all of the human body parts, the stomach is the most sensitive organ. The fact that it is often the most abused organ is an unfortunate reality. People can be very callous in filling the stomach with excess or poor-quality food and drink. In the modern day, people saturate their sacred temple (the human body) with numerous toxins such as recreational and allopathic drugs and narcotics, alcohol, tobacco and so on. This abuse creates deep-seated physical, mental and spiritual imbalances.

What is required for a healthy body and mind is the ingestion of the right quality of food at the right time and in the right quantity. There is a beautiful quote to further illustrate this point: "He who eats the right food knows no disease, and he who knows the right speech knows no quarrel." It is synonymous that he who eats the right food also instinctively knows right speech because speech directly represents the quality of our thoughts. The type of food we eat has a profound influence on our thoughts. Sattvic food creates healthy, harmonious, peaceful and elevating thoughts and speech. On the contrary, tamasic foods create vicious, negative and demonic thoughts and speech. What you are (in your physical health and mental disposition) is primarily determined by what kind of food you eat. The father of modern medicine, Hippocrates, gave the wise maxim, "Let your food be your medicine and your medicine be your food." There is really no greater health principle than this. Just as medicine is administered to the patient in right quality, quantity and at the right time to effect healing, likewise, food should be ingested in right quality, quantity and at the right time to create radiant health.

As explained earlier in the book, our bodily processes can be divided into three essential aspects. These three govern the entire metabolic process in the human body. The three processes are Agni (digestion), Ama and Mala (toxic waste and elimination) and *Rasayana* (rejuvenation of Ojas). It is the prana that regulates these activities in order of priority: first digestion, then elimination of metabolic waste and finally cellular rejuvenation.

The entire bodily process depends on prana. The flow of prana to any part of the body must not be disrupted or disturbed. If there is a blockage in the flow of prana, the body will suffer from some form of disease. When this prana leaves the body entirely, the result is death.

Chapter 15

The timing of healing

Everybody needs beauty as well as bread and places to play in and pray in where nature may heal and give strength to body and soul.

— John Muir

The question arises: when exactly does the healing take place? Healing takes place most effectively and fully when the body is resting or sleeping. However, you must provide the body with the right environment and circumstances for proper sleep. The most important factor is making sure that the stomach is completely empty by the time you go to bed. It is the primary responsibility of prana to attend to the digestion of food first. Only after digestion is complete will the prana attend to the other two important duties of removing ama and mala. Only then prana will tend to cellular regeneration. This evidently means that the process of digestion should occur during waking hours when the body is active. The last meal of the day should be finished at least three hours before sleep. If prana is busy digesting food all night long, it has no chance of eliminating ama and mala or performing rejuvenation.

This process is in harmony with the cycles of nature. During daylight or waking hours when the body is active, the digestive mechanism receives a natural impetus for the digestion process to take place smoothly. Obviously, when there is food in the stomach at bedtime and no physical activity while sleeping, the digestive process becomes sluggish or stops. This causes the food to remain in the stomach all throughout the night. This undigested food inevitably rots in the intestines, creating more ama.

Another harmful aspect about going to sleep with food in the stomach is that all the vital organs in the body will be denied fresh, new blood, especially the brain and the heart. They become immensely negatively affected as they need more than one third of the new blood supply for their efficient functioning. Furthermore, the other organs and bodily systems are denied their natural rejuvenation cycles. Having food in the stomach at bedtime is one of the quickest ways for chronic diseases to establish themselves in the body. When the stomach is empty at bedtime, the body is provided with the correct environment for prana to concentrate on its primary jobs. This allows the body to have its natural, daily internal servicing (cleansing and regeneration).

Chapter 16

The five pranic factors

Nature is our first Mother. She nurtures us throughout our lives. Our birthmother may allow us to sit on her lap for a couple of years, but Mother Nature patiently bears our weight our entire life. Just as a child is obligated to his birthmother, we should feel an obligation and responsibility toward Mother Nature. If we forget this responsibility, it is equal to forgetting our own Self. If we forget Nature, we will cease to exist, for to do so is to walk toward death.

— Amma

Forget not that the earth delights to feel your bare feet and the winds long to play with your hair.

— Khalil Gibran

There are five essential factors in manifesting and maintaining the harmonious flow of prana throughout the body.

1. Eradication of Vices
2. Mental Control
3. High-Quality Food

4. Exercise and Pranayama
5. Judicious Fasting

1. Eradication of vices

*Children, love can accomplish anything and
everything. Love can cure diseases. Love can heal
wounded hearts and transform human minds.
Through love, one can overcome all obstacles.*

— Amma

One who is seeking a happy and healthy life must make
sincere efforts in eradicating one's vices. Examples of
vices are not just the health-damaging habits of smoking, using drugs, drinking alcohol or gambling, which
are gross form of vices. There are other forms of vices as
well, like watching television, gossiping, over-eating or
emotional eating and reading nonproductive materials
like novels, tabloid magazines and newspapers. Actually, anything done repetitively that distracts us from
focusing on the Self can be called a vice. All these vices
drain the body of its prana. Wikipedia's definition of a
vice is, "A practice, behavior, or habit generally considered immoral, depraved or degrading in the associated
society." In more minor usage, vice can refer to a fault,
a negative character trait, a defect, an infirmity, or an

unhealthy habit (such as an addiction to smoking). Synonyms for vice include fault, depravity, sin, iniquity, wickedness and corruption. In short, any and all of those activities, which disrupt the harmony of prana, are a vice and must be eliminated for optimum health.

A person intent upon spiritual progress and success in life should cultivate a clear understanding of what causes good habits or virtues and bad habits or vices. Many of these bad habits can be attributed to our *samskaras* (latent tendencies/past karmas). Good karmas will create good habits or virtues, and bad karmas create bad habits or vices. Karma is created through our thoughts and actions. Karmas can be altered in the present by performing good actions with conscious awareness and dedication to the ultimate goal. There is a definite sequence to the manifestation of karma as explained by Stephen R. Covey in his book *The 7 Habits of Highly Effective People*, "Sow a thought; reap an action. Sow an action; reap a habit. Sow a habit; reap a character. Sow a character; reap your destiny."

Therefore, good character yields good karmas leading to all-around success, and bad character leads to vices causing only misfortune and suffering. Everyone should understand that even if one has performed wrong actions in the past, they can definitely change the present by exercising discrimination and a firm resolve to lead a noble and righteous life. It is basically self-inflicted suffering if one fails to live consciously with discrimination.

2. Mental control

When we live harmoniously with nature in love and unity, we will have the strength to overcome any crisis.

– Amma

The body and mind are inextricably linked. In fact, the physical body is basically the product and manifestation of the mind. If the physical body is healthy, the mind will also be strong and vice versa. A strong mind not only preserves and regulates the prana in the body but also draws prana from the cosmos into the body. In order to properly and completely gain control over the mind, it should be rid of all the negative emotions caused by the *shadripus* (six enemies that bind the soul to the process of birth and death and keep it confined in this material world, referred to as Maya or illusion). The shadripus are anger, jealousy, greed, lust, attachment and arrogance. The first three are said to pave the way toward *samsara* (the continuous cycle of birth and death). The shadripus quickly and profusely burn up the prana in the body just as a bundle of hay turns into ash in no time when set afire.

We must remember that everything is sentient; everything is full of consciousness and life. Everything exists in God. If we approach all situations with this attitude, then destruction becomes impossible for us. As humanity's intellect and scientific knowledge grow, we should not forget the feelings of the heart, which enable us to live in accordance with Nature and Her fundamental laws.

– Amma

Presently, the world is living in an age of the intellect. With all of the advancements in science, medicine and technology, life has become much more difficult on both the physical and mental planes. As a result of these hardships, the minds of people are becoming more and more burdened with stress, fear and uncertainty. These challenges are the cause of severe mental tension. This mental tension is the cause of chronic psychosomatic diseases. All these mental stressors leave the body vulnerable to acute diseases by drastically burning the body's natural resistance (ojas). Even modern researchers are beginning to admit that the state of mind has a profound impact on health. Their findings have revealed that tension and negative emotions persisting over a long period of time can impair the immune system, thus lowering the body's defenses against diseases. Clinical observations have revealed that the state of the mind changes the state of the body by working through the central nervous system, the endocrine system and the immune system.

Mental stress, according to Ayurveda, is caused by an overuse or wrong use of the mental faculties. If you perform intense mental work for many hours a day, or if you work long hours on the computer, these actions can cause an imbalance in prana, the mind-body conductor responsible for brain activity and the mind's energy. The first symptom of prana imbalance is losing the ability to cope with basic, daily stress. As the person becomes more stressed, the mind becomes hyperactive, and the person loses the ability to make clear decisions, think positively, feel enthusiastic and sleep soundly. To reduce chronic mental stress, one can control mental activity by monitoring what sensory input is allow to enter into one's minds from the television, radio, newspaper and computers. For example, if one is regularly upset after watching the nightly news, perhaps reducing the amount of television watched is a good idea.

Drug companies nowadays are making billions of dollars a year on new drugs to treat stress and stress-related diseases. These drugs only mask the symptoms of stress and often have many side effects. Ayurveda offers a much more holistic approach to help us cope with stress in a balanced way. Identifying sources of stress and becoming aware of its effects on our lives are essential in managing stress. There are many sources of stress, and there are equally as many possibilities of alleviating them. One should work toward the goals of eliminating the sources of stress and changing one's reactions to stress-provoking situations.

One may do this by practicing thoughtful responses to such situations rather than reacting automatically. Here are some helpful guidelines for putting this stress-relieving method into action:

• Be aware of your stressors and your emotional and physical reactions to them

• Recognize what is changeable and change it

• Reduce the intensity of your emotional reactions to stress

• Learn to moderate your physical reactions to stress

The five pranic factors

- Build up your physical reserves (ojas)
- Maintain your emotional reserves (prana)

The following are suggested practices from Ayurveda and Yoga to reduce stress in daily life

- *Yoga Nidra* (yogic sleep, a simple guided-meditation technique)
- Meditation (including Mantra Japa)
- Yoga
- Prayer
- Physical exercise
- Spending time in nature
- Listening to relaxing, peaceful music
- Massage
- Pranayama (gentle, relaxed, conscious breathing)
- Seva (selfless service) to the poor and needy
- Proper Diet (sattvic food)

Stress release begins with understanding what pushes you, what your major struggles are, how to put them into perspective, and how to make clear decisions on appropriate actions to take. Although modern society contributes to poor health in alarming ways, simple methods can be used to counteract negative influences and significantly improve health and vitality. Often, simple adjustments in diet and lifestyle can drastically improve our ability to cope with stress. Furthermore, practicing seva is one of the most effective ways of diverting the mind from personal burdens, thus relieving stress. People who work full-time jobs and still make time to do some volunteer work each week usually lead more fulfilling and less stressful lives.

Meditation

> *I only went out for a walk and finally
> concluded to stay out till sundown, for going
> out, I found, was really going in.*
>
> – John Muir

> *Meditation is the saving principle; it makes you
> immortal and eternal. Meditation takes you across the
> cycle of death and rebirth. Meditation is ambrosia.
> It actually prevents the fear of death. It makes you
> egoless and takes you to the state of no-mind. Once
> you transcend the mind, you cannot die. Meditation
> and spiritual practices give you the power and
> courage to smile at death. Meditation helps you
> see everything as a delightful play so that even the
> moment of death becomes a blissful experience.*
>
> – Amma (Awaken Children Vol.8 p 135-137)

The five pranic factors

The power of true meditation is unfathomable. Real meditation is simply the natural state of awareness or being. Meditation is the greatest way of keeping the mind still and clear. It promotes an optimistic outlook on life. A cheerful attitude and positive thinking promote strong mental health as well as physical well-being. The physical benefits of meditation are now being documented and utilized by the Western medical system. Meditation helps to normalize blood pressure, pulse rate and levels of stress hormones in the blood. It produces changes to the neuro hormones in the brain, creating a calming, nourishing effect. Meditation can raise pain-bearing capacity, eliminating dependency on painkillers that create numerous side effects. In addition to the clarity and sturdiness of mind gained through meditation, it lends an unwavering determination to overcome the shadripus.

Meditation is a state of true awareness. It allows one to realize that they are not the temporal, physical body subject to change from: birth, growth, old age, disease and, inevitably, death. Meditation also helps one to realize that one is not the mind that is constantly fluctuating from one thought or emotion to another– like happiness, sorrow, boredom, anger, jealousy and so on. True meditation will bring us to the state of awareness that we are *Paramatman* (The Supreme Consciousness), whose very nature is bliss that is absolute, infinite and changeless. In this state of awareness, all the disturbances pertaining to the body and the mind will instantly be reduced to nothingness just as burnt camphor leaves no trace. True meditation involves relaxing all the muscles and the mind from all the worldly thoughts and thinking unbrokenly about any aspect of divinity, God or of a *Sadguru* (perfect master). The unparalledled benefit of meditation is that it purifies the body, mind and the *chitta* (subconscious mind). Meditation gives the body radiant health, gives the mind clear reasoning power, and gives the chitta divine resolve. Thus, it liberates Atma-bala and transforms our whole life and consciousness from the human level to a divine level. It would be of great benefit to the world if everyone cultivated the habit of meditating at least one hour a day.

Meditation is the only truly worthwhile activity that one can ever perform as it will put you in direct touch with the never-ending source of joy and happiness. Through all of the vices and sense pleasures, this is actually what every human being is seeking consciously or unconsciously.

Amma says, *"Children, you should live with the remembrance of God. Your heart should constantly throb for God. There shouldn't be a single instant when you do not remember God. Constant thought directed to God is meditation, like the flow of a river. Do not waste time. Repeat your mantra while doing every action. Everyday, meditate for some time."*

3. High-quality food

Diet has a great deal of influence on our character. Children, you should take care to eat only simple, fresh, vegetarian food (sattvic food). The nature of the mind is determined by the subtle essence of the food we eat. Pure food creates a pure mind. Without forsaking the taste of the tongue, the taste of the heart cannot be enjoyed.

– Amma

Through her life and message, Amma reminds us that we are not the body; we are the Atma. Why bother to eat healthfully? Our bodies are vehicles for transporting the soul. Just as we would not put gasoline mixed with dirt into our cars, we should consider what type of fuel we put into our soul's vehicle. At the same time, we should be careful not to take our diets so seriously that we lose a sense of gratitude for whatever foods we receive. We are blessed if we have enough food to provide energy and nutrition because millions of people worldwide do not have this. Our thoughts and attitude during meals affect our digestion and assimilation as much as the food itself. We have infinite potential to heal the planet and ourselves by making some simple changes to our dietary habits. Every individual's food requirements will vary according to one's dosha and needs. Every person will have to choose the right quality of food that suits him or her, and it should be taken in the right quantity and at the right time.

The Ayurvedic diet not only nourishes the body but also restores the balance of the doshas, which is essential for maintaining health. An Ayurvedic diet is based on an individual's constitution. Medicine for one person may be poison for another. Each individual has unique dietary requirements; depending on one's dosha or constitutional type, some foods can be beneficial and others should be avoided. When choosing what to eat, one must consider the season, weather, time of day and quality of food as well as one's mental and emotional attitudes at the time of eating.

When we ingest food, we participate in the creative process of nature. Healthful food rejuvenates the cells of the whole body, especially our stomach lining and skin. How we eat also determines how food affects our body. If we feel emotionally imbalanced when we eat, our food may disrupt the body's natural order. If we overeat or eat too quickly, the poorly digested end product predisposes us to ill health. Food intake should contribute to order and coherence in the body. It should help us to stay balanced and boost our overall immunity.

Ahimsa ahara (non-violent diet)

Saving the lives of animals may save your own life. Extensive evidence shows that vegetarian and vegan diets are by far the healthiest diets. Scientific research is now proving that excessive consumption of the cholesterol and saturated fats found in animal products leads to heart disease and numerous forms of cancer. The consumption of animal products also leads to obesity, diabetes, hypertension, arthritis, gout, kidney stones and many other diseases. In addition, modern-day, factory-farming methods use hormones, antibiotics, chemical fertilizers and drugs to increase their output and profits. Commercial animal products contain high levels of herbicides and pesticides. When humans consume animal products, their bodies receive these poisons and become toxic. Since the 1960s, scientists have suspected that a meat-based diet is related to the development of arteriosclerosis and heart disease. As early as 1961, a study published in the *Journal of the American Medical Association* reported, "Ninety to ninety-seven percent of heart disease can be prevented by a vegetarian diet." Since that time, several well-organized studies have scientifically shown that, after tobacco and alcohol, the consumption of meat is the greatest single cause of mortality in Europe, the United States, Australia and other affluent areas of the world.

The human body is unable to process and utilize excessive amounts of animal fat and cholesterol, which accumulate on the inner walls of the arteries and constrict the flow of blood to the heart, resulting in high blood pressure, heart disease and strokes. Research during the past twenty years also strongly suggests a link between eating meat and cancer of the colon, rectum, breast and uterus. Another major concern about eating meat is that of chemical contamination. As soon as an animal is slaughtered, its flesh begins to putrefy, and after several days, it turns a sickly gray-green color.

The meat industry masks this discoloration by adding nitrites and other preservatives to give the meat a bright red color. Research now shows that most of these preservatives are carcinogenic.

Generally, Ayurveda encourages one to follow a pure, vegetarian diet. A yogic diet, similarly promotes sattva (purity) and ahimsa (non-violence). Killing animals for food is not only violence to animals. It is also harmful to the environment and all of the hungry people in the world due to the environmental pollution from slaughter houses and the large amount of natural resources needed to raise each factory animal. When an animal is killed, its body releases fear hormones and other toxins, which the meat-eater later ingests and absorbs into his or her body. That negative, emotional vibration then enters the person's consciousness. In addition, meat is dead; it is completely void of prana. As such, according to Ayurveda, meat creates tamas (dullness, darkness) in the mind and body.

Our task must be to free ourselves by widening
our circle of compassion to embrace all living
creatures and the whole of nature and its beauty.
Nothing will benefit human health and increase

Health and Consciousness
through Fasting and Cleansing

our chances of survival for life on earth as
much as the evolution to a vegetarian diet.

– Albert Einstein

Sattvic food

When food is pure, the mind is pure; this creates an
oasis for awakening and provides an awakening that
affects every level of our health (body-mind-spirit).

– Chandogya Upanishad, 6.5.1-4

Not a grain of the food we eat is made purely by our
own effort. What comes to us in the form of food is the
toil of our sisters and brothers, the bounty of nature and
God's compassion. Even if we have a million dollars,
we still need food to satisfy our hunger. After all, we
cannot eat dollars, so we should never eat anything
without first praying with a feeling of humbleness
and gratitude. Consider your food to be the Goddess
Lakshmi (the Goddess of Prosperity) and receive it with
devotion and reverence. Food is Brahman (the Supreme
Being). Eat the food as God's Prasad (blessed gift).

– Amma

Lord Krishna says in the *Bhagavad Gita* that there are
three qualities of food: sattvic food, rajasic food and

tamasic food. Yogis and *Sadhakas* (Spiritual Aspirants) should be careful to eat only pure sattvic food. Sattvic food gives excellent health to the body, quiets the mind's negative emotions and imparts calmness and power of concentration to the conscious mind. When the food is ingested, prana is set into action to take care of digestion of food. The digested food in turn liberates prana in the body. (It is like investing money to earn money). To create vibrant health, the amount of prana liberated should be more than the prana spent just as for the healthy functioning of a business enterprise, the selling price of a product should be reasonably more than the purchasing price. This excess prana helps keep the mind and all the vital organs of the body, along with the nervous system and the immune system, in excellent condition. This is why Ayurveda, saints, sages and Lord Krishna have all advocated eating only sattvic food for attaining the higher and supreme goals of life.

Rajasic and tamasic foods use more prana digesting the food than they give to the body, so these foods disturb the subconscious mind, keep the conscious mind restless (lacking in concentration and calmness) and leave the body vulnerable to diseases. Tamasic foods are the worst perpetrators, depleting the most amount of prana from the body. Rajasic and tamasic foods accelerate the aging process of the body.

In Ayurveda, emphasis is placed on a sattvic diet for healthy living. This is particularly important for keeping our minds clear, happy and at peace. The original sattvic diet was designed for the attainment of higher consciousness. Sattvic foods are foods that are abundant in prana. A sattvic diet means not only vegetarian food but also food rich in prana such as organic fresh fruits and vegetables. This requires avoiding canned food, processed food and foods prepared with chemical fertilizers or sprays. It also means eating properly prepared fresh foods. Foods prepared with lots of love become more sattvic. The ancient Ayurveda criteria for foods to be considered sattvic were quite simple: Foods were grown organically on good, rich fertile soil; foods were to be of attractive appearance and harvested at the correct time of year. Foods should be full of life force and enzymes and stay as close as possible to their natural, fresh state. In the modern world, we need to add to the following sattva criteria due to several other modern concerns. Sattvic foods should be grown without pesticides, herbicides, chemical fertilizers, hormones, irradiation or anything unnatural. Modern use of refinement processes and chemical additives, besides actually adding substances to our foods, depletes foods of their prana and leaves them lifeless. Sattvic foods are nutritive vegetarian foods like organic nuts, seeds, whole grains and fruits and vegetables that help build the brain tissue and develop Ojas. It takes time for the effects of dietary changes to manifest in the mind. Changing our diet may not impact our psychology overnight, but in a period of months, it can affect it significantly.

The person who always eats wholesome (sattvic)
food enjoys a regular lifestyle, remains unattached
to the objects of the senses, gives and forgives,
loves truth and serves others without disease.

– Ashtanga Hridayam

Sattvic food list

Fruits

Apples, Kiwi, Prunes, Apricots, Loquats, Tangerines, Bananas, Lychees, Pomegranates, Cantaloupes, Mangoes, Papayas, Cherries, Melons, Nectarines, Cranberries, Honeydew Melons, Oranges, Grapefruits, Watermelons, Pineapples, Grapes, Peaches, Plums, Guavas, Pears, Persimmons

Vegetables

Artichokes, Eggplants, Lettuce, Beets, Mustard Greens, Asparagus, Daikon Radishes, Onions, Endives, Fennel, Parsnips, Bok Choy, Peas, Broccoli, Green Beans, Potatoes, Brussels Sprouts, Kale, Radishes, Cabbage, Leeks, Lima Beans, Shallots, Carrots, Celery, Spinach, Cauliflower, Chard, Chanterelles, Sprouts, Corn, Squashes, Watercress, Turnips, Yams

Sprouted whole grains

Amaranth, Barley, Buckwheat, Bulgur, Millet, Quinoa

Rice

Basmati, Brown and Wild Rice.

Oils

Olive, Safflower, Sesame, Sunflower, Hemp, Flax and Chia.

Spices

Asafetida (hing), Coriander, Basil, Cumin, Nutmeg, Black Pepper, Fennel seed, Parsley, Cardamom, Fenugreek, Turmeric, Cinnamon, Cloves, Ginger

Nuts/seeds

Brazil nuts, Pumpkin seeds, Sunflower seeds, Hemp, Flax, Chia and Walnuts

Milks and cheese

Raw Organic Milk (un-pasteurized/un-homogenized) Seed milk, Hemp milk, Almond or other nut milk

Sweeteners

Cane juice, Raw honey, Stevia, Fruit Juices, Maple Syrup

Sattvic herbs

Organic herbs are used to directly support sattva in the mind and in meditation. Some of the most sattvic herbs include ashwagandha, bacopa, calamus, gotu kola, gingko, jatamansi, purnarnava, shatavari, saffron, shankhapushpi, tulasi and rose.

Rajasic food

Rajasic foods, or stimulant foods, are foods that agitate the mind and provoke mental restlessness. They are not completely beneficial, nor are they extremely harmful. Foods that cannot be categorized as either sattvic or tamasic are classified in this group. These foods often cause selfish, aggressive and dominating thoughts and actions, especially toward others. Stimulating foods energize and develop the individual consciousness and body but do not promote advancement of higher states of awareness or meditation.

Rajasic foods include beverages containing caffeine such as coffee and tea, carbonated beverages, soda and energy drinks, chocolate, spicy food, salt and fertilized eggs.

Tamasic Food

Consumption of tamasic or sedative foods are harmful to the body and mind. Foods that are harmful to the mind include anything that leads to a dull, sluggish, less-refined state of consciousness. Here "bodily harm" refers to all foods that cause detrimental or oxidative stress to the body directly or indirectly. Tamasic food stimulates and agitates the lower two chakras, increasing passion, desire, lust and the sense of individuality (ego). Tamasic food is detrimental to the refinement of higher awareness. In tamasic foods, there are three main forms of poison called the "Three White Poisons." These three poisons are white flour, white rice and white sugar. They cause immense detrimental harm to the body. They block the assimilation of all nutrients, at the same time leaching the body of its storehouse of vitamins, minerals and fiber. Since they are completely devoid of roughage, the feces become sticky and clog the colon, causing constipation. Remember, if low agni is the root cause of all diseases, constipation is the secondary cause of all diseases. Long-term buildup of ama can contribute to colon cancer, piles, irritable bowel syndrome and other complications.

Scientific research is now proving that excessive consumption of the cholesterol and saturated fats found in animal products leads to heart disease and numerous forms of cancer. The consumption of animal products also leads to obesity, diabetes, hypertension, arthritis, gout, kidney stones and many other diseases. In addition, modern-day factory farming methods use hormones, antibiotics, chemical fertilizers and drugs to increase their output and profits. Commercial animal products contain high levels of herbicides and pesticides. When humans consume animal products, their bodies receive these poisons and become toxic. The human body is unable to process and utilize excessive amounts of animal fat and cholesterol, which accumulate on the inner walls of the arteries and constrict the flow of blood to the heart. The results are often high blood pressure, heart disease and strokes. Research during the past twenty years also strongly suggests a link between eating meat and getting cancer of the colon, rectum, breast and uterus.

Tamasic foods include: meats, fish, eggs, onions, garlic, mushrooms, alcohol, blue cheese, opiates, stale or canned food.

Right quantity and right timing

The following are general principles that should be followed when eating. They will assure optimum digestion, assimilation and elimination. Never overeat. Half the stomach should be for food, a quarter for liquid, and the remaining portion for the movement of air. The less food you eat, the more mental control you will have. Do not sleep or meditate immediately after eating; if you do, you won't be able to digest the food properly. Always mentally repeat your mantra while you eat. This will purify the food and your mind at the same time.

– Amma

While Ayurveda gives specific amounts and times for eating, each individual will have to discover for himself or herself what is most suitable for them. The general guideline for eating the right quantity is to stop eating before you are full. In other words, you should not feel heaviness in the stomach after eating and never overeat. Overeating is one of the most harmful things one can do to their digestive system.

Eating guidelines that increase health

• Eat to about three-quarters of your capacity. Do not leave the table very hungry or very full.

• Avoid taking a meal until the previous meal has been digested. Allow approximately 3–6 hours between meals.

• Eat in a settled and quiet atmosphere. Do not work, read or watch TV during meal times. Avoid talking, if possible.

• Choose foods by balancing, physical attributes. In general, the diet should be balanced to include all six tastes: sweet, sour, salty, bitter, pungent and astringent. Follow specific recommendations according to your constitution. Each taste has a balancing effect, so including some of each minimizes cravings and balances the appetite and digestion. The general North American and European diet tends to have too much of the sweet, sour and salty tastes and not enough of the bitter, pungent and astringent tastes.

• Choose foods that are sattvic, whole, fresh, in-season and local foods.

• Yogurt, cheese, cottage cheese and buttermilk should be avoided at night.

• Follow food-combining guidelines.

• It is best not to cook with honey as it becomes toxic when cooked.

• Take a few minutes to sit quietly after each meal before returning to activity.

• Eat at optimal times for digestion: breakfast 7–9 a.m., lunch 10–2 p.m. and dinner 4–6 p.m.

• Wash face, hands and feet before meals.

• Rinse the mouth before and after eating.

• Dine in an isolated, neat and clean place. The environment should be pleasant. The eater should be in a comfortable, seated position.

• Eat only food prepared in a loving way. This method of food preparation increases the vitality-giving quality of the food.

• Chew food until it is an even consistency before swallowing.

• Hard items should be consumed in the beginning of the meal, followed by soft foods and subsequently liquids.

The five pranic factors

• Do not drink cold drinks just prior to or while eating. Also do not drink large quantities of liquids during meals for this habit weakens digestion. A few sips of warm water are okay with meals.

• Avoid heavy substances such as rich desserts after meals.

• Consumption of excessively hot food leads to weakness. Cold and dry foods lead to delayed digestion.

• Do not travel, perform vigorous exercise or engage in sexual intercourse within one hour after a meal as this will impede digestion. Walking (10–20 minutes) after a meal can help digestion.

• Avoid eating meals when thirsty and drinking water while hungry.

• Avoid eating meals immediately after exertion.

• Do not eat when there is not an appetite.

• Don't suppress the appetite as this leads to body pain, anorexia, lassitude, and vertigo and general debility.

• Don't suppress thirst as it leads to general debility, giddiness and heart disease.

Eating habits that decrease health

• Overeating
• Eating when not hungry
• Emotional eating

- Drinking juice or excess water while eating
- Drinking chilled water at any time
- Eating when constipated or emotionally imbalanced
- Eating at the wrong time of day
- Eating too many heavy foods or not enough light foods
- Snacking on anything except fruit in between meals
- Eating incompatible food combinations

Food-combining guidelines

Foods in **bold** lettering are listed first because they increase ama to such a degree that they should definitely be avoided.

Don't eat these foods	with these foods
Beans	fruit, cheese, eggs, fish, milk, meat, yogurt
Eggs	**milk**, fruit, beans, cheese, fish, kichari, meat, yogurt
Grains	fruit
Fruit	any other food, but dates with almonds are okay

Honey	and ghee by equal weight: avoid 1 tea-spoon honey with 3 teaspoons ghee (1 teaspoon each is okay). Ayurveda recommends that honey should not be cooked. When cooked, honey becomes sticky glue that adheres to mucous membranes and clogs the gross and subtle channels, producing toxins. Raw honey is considered to be amrita (nectar).
Hot Drinks	mangoes, cheese, fish, meat, starch, yogurt
Lemon	cucumbers, milk, tomatoes, yogurt
Melons	any other food, including other melons
Milk	**fruit especially bananas,** cherries, melons, and sour fruit, bread, fish, kichari, meat. Ayurveda also finds that pasteurized and/or homogenized dairy causes ama and is not recommended. Additionally, Ayurveda recommends consuming raw dairy and avoiding dairy produced in factory farms that use hormones, antibiotics, and steroids.

Nightshades (tomato, eggplant, bell pepper, potato)	cucumber, dairy products
Radishes	bananas, raisins, milk
Tapioca/ Yogurt	**milk**, fruit, cheese, eggs, fish, hot drinks, meat, nightshades

The Five Golden Rules for Maintaining Health

1. The stomach should be completely empty before going to sleep. The last meal of the day should be the smallest and lightest meal and completed at least three hours before going to sleep.

2. Drink 24-40oz. (750 ml-1.25 liter) of room temperature or warm water, depending on individual dosha/ constitution, first thing in the morning.

3. Never drink water soon after or along with the meals. Drink a small amount of warm water either half an hour before meals, if required, or two hours after.

4. Eat only when you are really hungry; otherwise, it is advised to reduce your meals.

5. Exercise suited to the individual's physical constitution is as important as eating the right food. Never ignore the importance of exercise.

Five Golden Rules Theory

There is a sufficiency in the world, in nature, for man's need but not for man's greed. ~Mohandas K. Gandhi

The primary reason for keeping the stomach empty at bedtime is that the prana is free to discharge its duty of elimination of ama and for cellular regeneration while the body is sleeping. This rule of keeping the stomach empty at bedtime is of exceptional importance for yogis, sadhaks, sanyasis and celibates who are serious in their sadhana. The greatest advantage of following this is that the sadhak arises with perfect alertness and superior concentration. The greatest obstacle for a sadhak, especially during meditation, is sleepiness and lack of concentration. One of the main reasons for this sluggishness is going to sleep with a full stomach.

Drinking plenty of water as soon as you wake up in the morning has an important purpose. The water is quickly absorbed into the blood stream and freely flows through the tiny capillaries of the body, effecting a thorough cleaning process and ensuring the supply of vital nutrients. A substantial quantity of pure water taken on an empty stomach is an excellent diuretic. In conjunction with keeping the stomach empty at bedtime, this is a great remedy to combat obesity. This is one of the most effective and natural ways of eliminating excess fat with little or no side effects.

There is a common complaint that drinking so much water in the morning causes bloating or nausea. This is primarily due to the presence of ama in the stomach from indiscriminately eating at night, followed by sleeping. One must understand that there is nothing more harmful for health than this habit of eating before sleeping. The nausea can be easily overcome if night meals are eliminated, or dinner is consumed at the correct time.

Drinking water during a meal or within two hours after a meal will quickly dilute the digestive enzymes. This greatly interferes with the whole digestive process. This is one of the major causes of obesity, flatulence and other stomach-related problems.

Eat only when the body is really hungry. Eating when the body is not hungry or before the previous meal has been completely digested creates confusion in the process of digestion as it depletes all of the prana. The result is that the digestive enzymes in the stomach get vitiated, causing acidity, flatulence, heart-burn, esophagus irritation and ulcers. Many modern health 'experts' believe that the stomach must never be kept empty, lest the acids in the digestive juices of the stomach will corrode the mucus lining of the stomach and duodenum, causing ulceration. They also believe eating when not hungry causes all the stomach-related problems like acidity, gastritis, distention, burning throat and esophagus and so on. The truth is all these disturbances take place only due to unremitting, poor eating habits over many years, giving no rest to the digestive system.

What people often fail to understand is, like every other living being in the world, humans need rest. This is absolutely essential for the efficient function of the body. Our digestive system also needs regular rest. Without proper rest, fatigue is sure to take a heavy toll. The stomach is the most sensitive organ of the body. Being so sensitive, the stomach has a precisely intelligent built-in regulatory mechanism. This self-regulating system does not just release acids to digest proteins on a whim. When fine-tuned, our stomach releases acidic juices in the right amount at the correct time, which paradoxically necessitates us to also eat food with intelligence and awareness.

Exercise is absolutely essential for health. If we take proper food and perform exercise daily, even that much is enough to ensure balanced health. Suitable exercise must be done till the end of our life. With proper exercise, the vital organs, muscles and bones are strengthened. Exercise prevents one from becoming a victim of a host of old-age diseases such as osteoporosis, Parkinson's disease and Alzheimer's disease.

Following The Five Golden Rules does not involve the administration of any medicines or any other kind of treatment. The body can often heal any imbalances of health on its own. All we have to do is to provide the body with the right environment. We need to realize that our body has enormous capacity for healing and rejuvenation when provided with the right opportunity. It can do a perfect healing job, better than the best healer, armed with the best healing techniques and supplemented by modern equipment and gadgets. God has created this human form; therefore, it can never be anything but perfect. God is residing in this human body as Atma. Then how can it fall ill? The reasonable answer is: It is only when we abuse this body through "wrong living and wrong thinking" that the body becomes a victim of innumerable diseases. In fact, the human body is the most precise, precious and wonderful mechanism that was ever made in creation. It is not meant to suffer the way people are suffering today from so many diseases, in utter despair and helplessness.

When To Eat?

The Ayurvedic physician begins the cure of disease by arranging the diet that is to be followed by the patient. The Ayurvedic physicians rely so much on diet that it is declared that all diseases can be cured by following dietetic rules carefully along with the proper herbal supplements, but if a patient does not attend to his diet, a hundred good medicines will not cure him.

– Charaka Samhita, 1.41

There is a saying in Ayurveda and Yoga: "He who eats once a day is a Yogi; he who eats twice a day is a *bhogi* (one who loves to enjoy life); he who eats three times a day is a *rogi* (a patient or a patient in the making), and he who eats more than three times daily is literally digging his own grave through his teeth."

Health and Consciousness
through Fasting and Cleansing

One essential rule for maintaining balanced health is eating only when the body is truly hungry. If this rule is ignored, it will eventually lead to many digestion-related problems such as chronic indigestion, irritable bowel syndrome, loose motion, constipation, burning of the stomach and esophagus, gastritis, peptic ulcers, a bloated feeling in the stomach and a general feeling of lack of enthusiasm and interest in life. These are warning signs for the onset of chronic diseases in the future. One needs to gain the sensitivity of identifying true hunger versus false hunger. There are three kinds of hunger: physiological hunger, psychological hunger and epicurean hunger. Of the three types of hunger, only the first kind of hunger is true hunger. The other two are false or self-hypnotic hunger. True physiological hunger can be felt by those who are engaged in hard physical labor or exercise such as going to the gym, martial arts, sports and yoga. Those whose work environment or lifestyle is sedentary are more likely to experience false hungers.

Psychological hunger is a false hunger, which is characterized by time schedule and routines. The mind has been trained by society, the family or doctor that the body must eat breakfast, lunch, dinner and snacks as per a time schedule. People eat whether or not there is hunger. The concept that one must eat at a predetermined time is entirely wrong and harmful. For proper digestion, assimilation and elimination, one must eat only when there is true hunger. If one is bound by the time constraints such as work or school, then the earlier meal must be adjusted so that the stomach is empty at least an hour before the next meal. This is very important so that the digestive mechanism will benefit from proper rest for efficient functioning.

Psychological hunger is also referred to as emotional eating. Most people don't just eat simply to satisfy hunger. Humans turn to food for emotional and psychological comfort, stress relief or a reward. Unfortunately, this type of emotional eating doesn't fix any problems. It usually creates more problems, making you feel worse. The original emotional issue remains, and the feeling of guilt sets in for overeating. Furthermore, the body becomes lethargic. Learning to identify emotional eating triggers is the primary step to breaking free from food cravings and compulsive overeating.

Epicurean hunger is the most harmful kind of hunger as it is born out of greed for eating tasty dishes.

It is a form of pure hedonism. When the mind sees a tasty dish that it likes, there is an instant reaction of false hunger. This is actually a neurological response that compels one to devour food. This is a guaranteed recipe for disaster by destroying the digestive system as well as any sensibility of mind. One who is a *Bhogi* (one who eats or lives to enjoy the senses alone) will be burdened by illness.

One must develop the sensitivity and awareness to clearly identify true and false hunger. If one is not really hungry, it is clearly wise to skip that meal. There is a sure way to develop this sensitivity, but first we have to understand what destroys the sensitivity. When people develop the bad habits of snacking or drinking tea or coffee indiscriminately between meals, the body loses its sensitivity and is never sure when the stomach is empty. Snacking or drinking between meals should be avoided except for pure room temperature water or warm water with fresh lemon juice, sweetened with a little honey or jaggery (only after two hours of eating your meals). If this guideline is followed, the body will quickly develop the sensitivity to identify true hunger.

4. Exercise and pranayama

*Just as nature creates the favorable circumstances
for a coconut to become a coconut tree, and for
a seed to transform itself into a huge fruit tree,
nature creates the necessary circumstances through
which the individual soul can reach the Supreme
Being and merge in eternal union with Him.*

— Amma

Both vibrant health and Self-realization come through discipline and awareness. Yogis undergo many austerities to attain liberation. To raise our level of health and consciousness, it is essential to control unrestrained desires and drives. Integration of *dinacharya* (daily routine) is an important step in cultivating discipline and awareness.

Din means "day," and *acharya* means "to follow, to find, close to." To follow or be close to the day implies unifying your daily routine with the natural cycle of the sun, moon, earth and the other planets. Following the dinacharya is one of the best means to align with nature. This creates balance and prevents disease. Ultimately, one will find that health and happiness are truly one's most natural state.

The rishis considered daily routine to be a stronger healing force than any other curative medicine. Today, society is out of touch with nature. For example, on any given day, very few people know where the moon is in its cycle. In order for us to really heal, we must re-attune ourselves to nature's cycles.

Properly performed exercise produces both physical health and mental happiness. To avoid harm, exercise should be tailored to one's age and dosha. For most people, yoga asana and breathing exercises (pranayama)

124

are ideal. Additionally, walking, swimming, tai chi, chi kung and bicycling are good for most people. Early morning exercise is especially beneficial as it removes stagnation in the body-mind, strengthens the digestive fire, reduces excess fat and gives an overall feeling of lightness and joy. It also fills the body and mind with prana.

Proper exercise and pranayama are equally as important as eating the right food. We are hearing more and more of people getting afflicted with various chronic diseases, especially obesity. It is mainly due to a lack of physical exercise compounded by the wrong food. With the numerous advancements in science and technology, people's lives have become physically so much easier, but, mentally, life has become harder. As a result of this over-burden of the mind, people are looking to other outlets for release instead of physical exercise. This is a serious cause of disease. Everyone needs to cultivate a daily exercise routine. This will assure that one will stay physically fit and maintain mental health until the end of life. Even Gandhi was doing yoga until his death. One should exercise until the body breaks a sweat. This allows for the proper flow of prana and energizes every cell in the body. However, vigorous exercise is not recommended for very weak and emaciated people, after heavy meals, or for anyone with a febrile condition. It is also contraindicated for people who have a tendency to bleed, tuberculosis, heart diseases, asthma or vertigo.

Surya Namaskar and Yoga

> *By asana, one avoids diseases; by pranayama,
> one avoids adharma; and by pratyahara, the
> Yogi controls his or her mental activity.*
>
> — *Yoga Chudamani, verse 109*

Creating a personal hatha yoga sadhana is extremely helpful on the path of Self-realization. As explained previously, Ayurveda and yoga are very closely aligned. Yoga is important for dissolving physical tension and calming the mind before meditation. It is the perfect ayurvedic exercise because it rejuvenates the body, improves digestion and removes stress. It can be done by anyone of any age. Yoga asana can balance all of the three doshas. Yoga tonifies every area of the body and cleanses the internal organs of toxins, which is one of the goals of Ayurveda. Yoga practices are most beneficial when tailored to support the individual's dosha, state of health and lifestyle. Asana should be practiced under the guidance of an experienced teacher. According to Ayurveda, there are three main reasons for performing yoga asanas: as exercise for a healthful living regime, as therapy to treat specific disorders in the body and mind, and as a means to return the doshas to their natural state. The ultimate purpose of yoga is spiritual growth and advancement. Scientific research is now proving that hatha yoga can assist in healing various diseases including arthritis, asthma, back pain, constipation, diabetes, diarrhea, digestive disorders, emotional and mental disorders, heart disease, hormonal imbalances, hypertension, immune weakness, insomnia, migraine headaches, neck pain, physical and mental fatigue, scoliosis, stress, thyroid disorders and numerous conditions.

Hatha yoga enhances physical health through numerous methods. It strengthens muscles, maintains joint and spine flexibility and integrity, and balances the subtle anatomy (chakras, nadis and koshas). Furthermore, yoga relaxes, rejuvenates, strengthens and energizes the whole body and mind by tonifying and nourishing all of the body systems. Yoga assists in cleansing on all levels of being. On the mental and emotional levels, it harmonizes and stills one's thoughts, bringing self-awareness to the emotional processes. Yoga practice becomes a mirror in which one can examine the Self.

Surya Namaskar

> *By a continual practice of yoga for three months, the purification of the nadis takes place. When the nadis have become purified, certain external signs appear on the body of the Yogi. They are lightness of the body, brilliancy of complexion, increase of the agni and leanness of the body, and along with these, absence of restlessness in the body.*
>
> — Yoga Tattva, verses 44-46

Surya Namaskar (Sun Salutations) is, in and of itself, a complete yogic exercise. It blesses the body by giving the benefit of all yogasanas while incorporating natural pranayama. It can be done in cycles from 12 to 108 depending upon the physical fitness level of the individual. Surya Namaskar done in a traditional way, as prescribed by yogic texts, should be performed at the time of sunrise, facing the sun and letting its rays fall freely on the body. Traditionally, there are 12 poses involved in one Surya Namaskar, and every pose will be accompanied by the chanting of each of the 12 names of the Sun god. Doing Surya Namaskar in a traditional way may not be possible for many due to various practical difficulties. Such persons may do them at any convenient time on an empty stomach. In this case, they do not need to chant the 12 names of the Sun god. The mantras *MA* (symbolizing divine love) and *OM* (symbolizing divine light) can be silently infused with the ingoing and outgoing breath. Ma belongs to the *Puraka* (inhalation), and Om belongs to the *Rechaka* (exhalation).

Basic Surya Namaskar Mantra and Instruction

Position 1:

Om Mitraya Namaha
(Prostrations to Him who is affectionate to all.)
Start in a standing position, facing the sun. Both your feet should touch each other, palms joined together in prayer pose.

Position 2:

Om Ravaye Namaha
(Prostrations to Him who is the cause of change.)
With a deep inhalation, raise both arms above your head and tilt slightly backward, arching your back.

Position 3:

Om Suryaya Namaha
(Prostrations to Him who induces activity.)
With a deep exhalation, bend forward and touch the
mat, both palms in line with your feet, forehead touching your knees.

Position 4:

Om Bhanave Namaha
(Prostrations to Him who diffuses light.)
With a deep inhalation, take your right leg away from
your body in a big, backward step. Both your hands
should be firmly planted on your mat, your left foot
between your hands, head tilted towards the ceiling.

Position 5:

Om Khagaya Namaha
(Prostrations to Him who moves in the sky.)
With a deep inhalation, take your right leg away from
your body in a big, backward step. Both your hands
should be firmly planted on your mat, your left foot
between your hands, head tilted toward the ceiling.

Position 6:

Om Pushne Namaha
(Prostrations to Him who nourishes all.)

With a deep exhalation, shove your hips and butt up toward the ceiling, forming an upward arch. Your arms should be straight and aligned with your head.

Position 7:

Om Hiranyagarbhaya Namaha
(Prostrations to Him who contains all wealth.)
With a deep exhalation, lower your body down until your forehead, chest, knees, hands and feet are touching the mat, your butt tilted up. Take a normal breath in this pose.

Position 8

Om Marichaye Namaha
(Prostrations to Him who possesses rays.)
With a deep inhalation, slowly snake forward till your head is up, your back arched and concave as much as possible.

Position 9:

Om Adityaya Namaha
(Prostrations to Him who is the Son of Aditi.)
Exhaling deeply, again push your butt and hips up toward the ceiling as in position 6, arms aligned straight with your head.

Position 10:

Om Savitre Namaha
(Prostration to Him who is fit to be worshipped.)
Inhaling deeply, bring your right foot in toward your body in a big, forward step. Both your hands should be planted firmly on your mat, right foot between your hands, head tilted toward the ceiling.

Position 11:

Om Arkaya Namaha
(Prostrations to Him who is the reproducer of everything.)
Exhaling deeply, rise up and touch the mat, keeping both your palms in line with your feet, forehead touching your knees.

Position 12:

Om Bhaskaraya Namaha
(Prostrations to Him who is the cause of luster.)
Inhaling deeply, raise both your arms above your head and tilt slightly backward.
Return to stand facing the sun, both feet touching, palms joined together in prayer pose.

Practical Benefits of Surya Namaskar

• Surya Namaskar is a workout for the muscles, joints, ligaments and the skeletal system by improving posture and balance. The limbs become symmetrical while the internal vital organs are massaged and become more functional.

• Surya Namaskar is beneficial for a healthy digestive system. Yoga poses increase blood flow to the digestive tract and stimulate peristalsis so that digestion is more efficient. Yoga is calming, which relaxes the digestive system and leads to more effective and efficient elimination.

• Surya Namaskar helps to cope with insomnia and other sleep-related disorders as it calms the mind.

• Surya Namaskar practice regulates hormones and irregular menstrual cycles.

• Surya Namaskar increases blood circulation.

• Surya Namaskar helps to burn calories and stay fit. Practicing Surya Namaskar is one of the easiest ways to stay in shape. It stretches the abdominal muscles. Regular practice helps to lose excessive belly fat and gives a flat stomach. The asanas in Surya Namaskar stimulate sluggish glands to increase their hormonal secretions.

The thyroid gland especially has a huge effect on weight balance as it affects body metabolism.

• Surya Namaskar adds a glow to the face, making facial skin radiant and ageless. It is a natural solution to prevent the onset of wrinkles. Overall, yoga is excellent for the skin.

• Surya Namaskar boosts one's natural endurance. It promotes ojas (vitality and strength). It also reduces the feelings of restlessness and anxiety.

• Surya Namaskar makes the whole body more flexible, especially the spine and limbs.

• Surya Namaskar regulates the pineal gland and hypothalamus to prevent pineal degeneration and calcification. It opens the 72,000 nadis, which are the body's yogic energy meridians.

Other Exercises

Swimming, cycling, jogging and walking are excellent exercises. Skipping is an exercise, which can be done with a great health advantage to keep fit and energetic. Skipping is one of the cheapest, most effective fat-burning workouts you can do, and it does not require much space; it's fun too. It can be done outside in nature as well as in the home in a well-ventilated room. It is a superb exercise for the heart, lungs and blood circulation. If it is done properly, it can give the same benefit of one hour of walking or half an hour of jogging in as little time as only five minutes. However, people with poor lungs, a weak heart or arthritis should first consult an expert. Walking is a universal exercise as it is suitable for people of all ages and genders.

Among all the forms of exercises, yogasanas are the best as they can beautifully harmonize the flow of prana to all the body parts as no other exercises can. They take care of all the vital organs, nerves, spine and the brain. Apart from this, they bring peace to the mind and calmness to the subconscious mind, hence they are considered spiritual exercises.

Pranayama

Children, when you sit for meditation, do not think that you can still your mind immediately. At first, you should relax all parts of your body. Loosen your clothes if they are too tight. Make sure that the spine is erect. Then close your eyes and concentrate your mind on your breath. You should be aware of your inhalation and exhalation. Normally we breathe in and out without being aware of it, but

Health and Consciousness
through Fasting and Cleansing

*it should not be like that; we should become aware
of the process. Then the mind will be wakeful.*

– Amma

Pranayama is the practice of controlling our "life force" or *prana*. In hatha yoga, pranayama includes specific breathing exercises that assist in maintaining the health of the body and achieving deep inner awareness through stilling the mind. Pranayama leads to inner peace, tranquility and steadiness of mind and good health. Asana and pranayama usually go hand in hand. A simple form of pranayama is the repetition of mantras along with the inhalation and exhalation. For example, one can practice the *MA-OM* meditation technique. Silently repeat *MA* while breathing in and *OM* while breathing out. Focus internally on the vibration of the sound. As we repeat this type of pranayama, the breath and the sound vibration unite as one to take the yogi into deep states of meditation, and the stillness of consciousness dawns. It should be noted that Amma advises that complex pranayama exercises should only be practiced under the guidance of a competent master.

Pranayama is usually associated with some sort of breathing exercise. In reality, what it means is to invigorate or expand the prana in the body and gain complete control over it. In yogic terms, this involves some special breathing processes. The breathing process is the medium, and gaining control of prana is the goal. The need for doing pranayama has become more and more a necessity as the pollution levels in towns and cities has risen to alarming levels. It is of vital importance to properly oxygenate the blood and eliminate the toxic substances. Anybody above the age of 10 years can do simple pranayama without *Kumbhaka* (breath retention). *Anuloma-viloma* (alternate nostril breathing) and *Kapalabhati* (rapid exhalation) as well as simple, deep abdominal breathing can be done to enhance the pranic level in the body. Pranayama should be done on an empty stomach and only under the guidance of an expert.

5. Judicious fasting

Fasting is a natural method of healing. When animals or savages are sick, they fast.

– Paramahansa Yogananda

Health and Consciousness through Fasting and Cleansing

Fasting is the greatest remedy- the physician within.
~ Philippus Paracelsus, one of the three fathers of
Western medicine

The best of all medicines is resting and fasting.
— Benjamin Franklin

Fasting is the single greatest natural healing therapy. It is nature's ancient, universal 'remedy' for many problems.
— Dr. Elson Haas, M.D., Staying Healthy with
Nutrition

Judicious fasting is one of the greatest ways of harmonizing prana in the body. Fasting helps in overcoming numerous physical ailments. Ayurveda attaches great importance to regular fasting. Ayurveda texts say *"Langhanam paramoushadham;"* fasting is the supreme medicine to overcome all diseases, acute or chronic. Fasting also increases mental control and power. Fasting has been called a "miracle cure" because of the vast number of physical conditions it improves. Cited most often are allergies, arthritis, digestive disorders of all kinds, skin conditions, cardiovascular disease and asthma.

The five pranic factors

Shankya philosophy says that the human soul is encased in *Panchamaya koshas* (five sheaths or covers). They are *annamaya kosha* (gross/food sheath), *pranamaya kosha* (vital life-force sheath), *manomaya kosha* (mental sheath), *vijnanamaya kosha* (knowledge sheath) and *anandamaya kosha* (bliss sheath). The minds of people who do not do sadhana dwell in the gross, physical plane, annamaya kosha. Their minds are so gross that if they miss even one meal, they feel ill. It is because their minds are not subtle enough to understand that the body is actually sustained by prana, which in reality is under the jurisdiction of the mind. Great mental control can be attained through regular fasting. Fasting has a far-reaching salutary effect not just on the body and mind but also even on the chitta. The rishis say judicious fasting has an amazing power to rid the body of toxins and mental impurities. Fasting also helps to remove negative samskaras, which is termed as *Chitta Shuddhi* (impurities of the sub-conscious). That is why Ayurveda and Yoga consider fasting as a sacred discipline leading to Self-Realization.

Many modern doctors are ignorant about the virtues of fasting. Many people believe fasting weakens the body, mind and spirit. Truly, indiscriminate fasting is harmful just as indiscriminate eating is dangerous, but judicious fasting is as virtuous as judicious eating. The point is to have a balanced attitude coupled with awareness. Pregnant women, nursing mothers, malnourished people and individuals with cardiac arrhythmias, renal or liver problems are advised not to fast.

The Virtue of Fasting

> *"Prayer brings us halfway to God; fasting
> takes us to the gateway of Heaven."*
>
> – Muhammad

Normal people who do not do any sadhana depend entirely upon food for sustenance, so their minds are bound to food alone for generating prana. There's no problem with enjoying food, but excess food on a regular basis creates a burden for the body. As mentioned earlier, the prana in the body helps digest the food, and the digested food liberates additional prana in the body. In fact, prana is not just within our body but all around us just like air is not just within our lungs but all around us. Prana is all-pervading throughout the universe.

Fasting is an excellent antidote for our over-indulgences. When the mind is detached from unreasonable dependency upon food alone as the sole source of prana through judicious fasting, it gains strength and begins to draw prana into the body from the ultimate, cosmic source. Fasting is not only good for sadhaks but also for ordinary people to strengthen their minds to pursue their professions efficiently and successfully.

Humans have fasted as a spiritual practice since ancient times. Modern research is now proving that fasting has many health benefits. This research is showing that short fasts, lasting anywhere from 20 to 36 hours, can reduce many risk factors involved in heart disease, diabetes and even cancer.

Forgoing food for several hours does not cause the metabolism to slow down, nor does it create disturbances in blood sugar levels. In fact, the opposite is true; short fasts improve insulin sensitivity. When cells are sensitive to the effects of insulin, they do a substantially better job modulating blood sugar levels after meals, and this makes the job of the pancreas much easier. Loss of insulin sensitivity is a risk factor for both heart disease and diabetes. Short fasts also reduce oxidative stress and inflammation in cells. This helps prevent and repair DNA damage that could otherwise develop into cancer. Other research suggests that fasting slows the aging process. In other words, fasting can help us to live longer by maintaining and restoring our organs. Intermittent fasting is quickly being embraced as an anti-aging strategy. Intermittent fasting means fasting one day a week or three consecutive days in a month.

Healing Benefits of Fasting

"Fasting is the soul's nourishment. It reigns in language and seals one's lips. It tames desire and calms the choleric temperament. It awakens consciousness, renders the body docile, dispels nightly dreams, cures headaches and strengthens the eyes."

– John Chrysostom, Founding Christian Minister

• **Fasting Promotes Detoxification.** Processed foods contain numerous additives. These additives may become *ama* in the body. Most of these toxins are stored in fats. Fat is burnt during fasting, especially when it is prolonged and toxins get released. The liver, kidneys, colon, blood and other organs in the body get proper detoxification.

• **Fasting Rests the Digestive System.** During fasting, the digestive organs rest.

• **Fasting Resolves Inflammatory Response.** Modern researchers are finding that fasting promotes the resolution of inflammatory diseases and allergies. Examples of such inflammatory diseases are rheumatoid arthritis and skin diseases such as psoriasis.

• **Fasting Reduces Blood Sugar.** Fasting increases breakdown of glucose so that the body can get energy. It reduces production of insulin, resting the pancreas. Glucagon is produced to facilitate the breakdown of glucose, thus the outcome of fasting is a reduction in blood sugar.

• **Fasting Increases Fat breakdown.** Fasting promotes ketosis. This is the breakdown of fats to release energy. The fats stored in the kidney and muscles are broken down to release energy.

• **Fasting Alleviates High Blood Pressure.** Fasting is one of the best ways of reducing blood pressure. It reduces the risk of atherosclerosis. Atherosclerosis is the clogging of arteries by fat particles.

• **Fasting Promotes Weight Loss.** Fasting promotes rapid and effective weight loss by reducing the store of fats in the body.

• **Fasting Promotes a Healthy Diet.** Fasting reduces the craving for artificial and processed foods by promoting the desire for natural foods, especially water and fruits.

• **Fasting Helps Conquer Addictions.** Research is also showing that fasting helps addicts reduce their cravings for nicotine, alcohol, caffeine and other commonly abused substances.

• **Mental and Emotional Benefits of Fasting.** Fasting greatly improves mental clarity and focus. With renewed mental clarity, there is greater freedom, flexibility and energy to do the projects that are important to you. Emotionally, the mind will feel calmer, clearer and happier. Fasting helps to overcome depression and achieve goals. Fasting helps to improve concentration, reduce anxiety, promote sound sleep and awaken with a refreshed feeling.

• **Fasting Increases Immunity.** Just as impure gold is rendered pure by melting it in the crucible again and again, so also this impure mind is rendered purer by repeated fasting. There is an age-old saying: "prevention is better than a cure." The greatest method of prevention is through improving the body's natural immunity. Fasting is one of the most effective ways of preventing both acute and chronic diseases. During the period of fasting, the prana is free from the burden of digestion. Therefore, it is free to carry out inner cleansing of metabolic waste and cellular regeneration. After

144

one has become used to the new regimen of eating as per the dietary rules mentioned in this book, one can introduce fasting one day a week. Following the simple dietary rules and fasting one day a week, the body's immunity will always remain strong.

Signs of proper cleansing:
1. Improvement in quality of sleep
2. Improvement of energy and vitality
3. Less sluggishness in the morning
4. Clear complexion
5. Improvement of digestion (assimilation and elimination)
6. Sattvic quality of mind
7. Clear and concise thinking
8. Overall body comfort

Excessive cleansing and fasting can easily lead to a depletion of ojas and increase of Vata dosha.

Signs that it is not the proper cleanse or that the cleanse was too long:
1. Aggresiveness, anxiety, lethargy
2. Feeling "spaced out"
3. Cold extremities
4. Waking during the night

5. Bloating and gas
6. Constipation
7. Loss of appetite
8. Fatigue
9. Body aches and/or popping or cracking of the joints

If you're fasting or cleansing for the first time, it is normal to feel the detox effects of caffeine, alcohol, sugar, meat or other addictive substances. It varies completely from person to person. If in two or three days these detoxification symptoms haven't passed and you're still not feeling some of the good cleansing signs, then some adjustments may need to be made.

Preparing The Body and Mind For Fasting

Withdraw the senses and fix the mind on God. Pray to God to guide you and to throw a flood of light on your spiritual path. Say with feeling: "O God, guide me! Protect me; protect me! I am Thine; I am Thine! Forsake me not!" You will be blessed with purity, light and strength.

– Swami Sivananda

One needs to first have a clear understanding that fasting is not torture or denial. It is a rewarding practice to gain mastery over the body and mind. What usually discourages one from the practice of fasting is the current state of tamas in the body and mind. The mind has become completely addicted to eating tasty foods any time and anywhere it wants, giving little or no regard for the body's hunger. In this scenario, the body has habituated itself to consuming more food than is actually required.

When the body is overloaded with toxic waste, the mind feels repulsed by the concept of fasting. The reason is that the nerves have become used to functioning in an unnatural state of toxicity and find the new environment of fasting too much. Fasting clears out the toxicity in a rapid manner, causing the nerves to become irritable. This is quite similar to what happens to the nervous system of a drug addict or alcoholic reacting when they are abruptly denied that substance. The cleaner the body is, the easier it is to fast. Therefore, one has to rid the body of the toxic matter by following the five golden rules mentioned later in this book. Then it becomes easy and joyful to fast.

One of the benefits of fasting is the effect it has on our emotional wellbeing. One is likely to feel more emotional during and directly after fasting. This isn't a negative aspect; it's actually a positive one as it provides an opportunity for cleaning out old, stagnant and negative emotional patterns. This is also one reason why it's so important to slow down during a fast. To be free of the usual daily obligations allows time for inner discovery. One can start with a simple, short-term fast. Short fasts will help one enjoy the many benefits of fasting, allowing the body, digestive tract and organs a chance to rest and repair and heal. This also allows rest for the weary mind and a chance for one to begin the process of rebuilding the inner connection to the Higher Self. The benefits of fasting reach into every aspect of our lives. Whether fasting for increased health or increased mental clarity, both will eventually come. Fasting can be an ongoing practice like a seed sprouting, developing and bearing fruit over time, providing a bounty of healing benefits.

Fasting one day per week and observing other health rules can prevent the onset of acute conditions. The greatest advantage in fasting is that you are not dependent on any external agents like drugs or other treatments for rejuvenation. You are allowing your body's inner powers to take charge of the healing. In other systems of healing when the wrong drug is administered owing to wrong diagnosis or mistakenly, or even when taking the right drug in the wrong quantity or potency, the disease may increase. Other previously non-existent symptoms may also manifest. Indiscriminate use of antibiotics can seriously harm the body's natural immune system. Improper use of steroids can cause even irreparable damage to vital organs. When antibiotics are not administered systematically or due to negligence on the part of the patients, then there is the likelihood of the microbes or the viruses developing resistance to the drugs. Then it becomes very difficult to treat. They may become what is called a "super bug," meaning they are not responsive to antibiotics anymore.

In preparation for a fast, keep in mind that the toughest part of a fast is simply beginning it. Prepare for a fast by eating fewer and lighter meals for a couple days prior. The length of preparation is based on the intensity and length of your planned fast. The longer or more intense the fast, the more days of preparation you should make. For a one-day fast, you can just eat a light dinner the night before. Depending on the type of fast, drink one to four quarts of water per day. Use the purist quality water available or distilled water.

Those undertaking a pure water fast may add a slice of lemon to the water as it adds a little flavor as well as beneficial enzymes and is cleansing in nature.

During the fast, it is essential to allow ample opportunity for rest, both physical and emotional. Prepare in advance to have enough quiet time in your schedule during the fasting period. Reading is an ideal activity, especially if the material is uplifting. Give yourself permission to take short naps if needed. One should take great care to avoid emotionally upsetting circumstances. Light exercise, like walking in nature, yoga or stretching is fine as long as you are not exhausted. Many spiritual paths encourage silence on the chosen fasting day or days. This allows for the pranic reserves to increase and stabilize. Dry skin brushing further enhances the body's ability to detox through the skin and the lungs. Those who are filled with ama in the colon may choose to have colonics or some type of herbal laxatives in order to assist in the cleansing process. More will be discussed later on this subject.

If one is preparing for a longer fast, then a modified diet is encouraged. For a three-day fast, eating only fresh fruits and vegetables for two or three days prior is advisable. If the fast is going to be longer, for every day one plans to fast, that many days of pure fruit and vegetables should be taken prior to the fast.

Length of Fasting

The period of time one can fast depends upon the current health condition and dosha as well as current emotional, mental and spiritual needs. Most people with no chronic health conditions can fast one day a week with immense health benefits. Those who are mentally and physically strong can fast three days continuously on water and fruit or vegetable juices at up to four times a year. The best time to do a three-day fast is on the equinoxes and solstices (the changing of the seasons). Longer fasts may be undertaken with the guide of a medical expert or spiritual master. These fasts may be seven, ten, fourteen, twenty-one or twenty-eight days in length.

Once you have become accustomed to fasting, you will discover that even during a three-day fast you will not feel weak. Rather you will feel that you are sustained by prana. One may even attend to all normal regular duties without feeling tired. This fast will completely overhaul your system just as an automobile is thoroughly serviced at a service station. The knowledge, perseverance and inspiration to do this successfully come from regular, dedicated sadhana, especially mantra japa and meditation.

If you are a sadhak, you can align the day of your fasting (it can be any convenient day of the week) to your Guru, (if you have a Guru) or to your *Ishta Devata* (beloved form of God/Goddess) or family deity. For instance, Monday is considered to be the day of Lord Shiva, Thursday is the day of the Guru, Friday is related to Goddess Lakshmi and Saturday is the day of Lord Hanuman. Doing so, you would then be dedicating or sanctifying your fast. If you are fasting for astrological purposes, each day is governed by one of the planets. Sunday is the day of the sun, Monday is the day of the Moon, Tuesday is ruled by Mars, Wednesday corresponds to Mercury, Thursday is for Jupiter, Friday is for Venus and Saturday is ruled by Saturn. You should also try to be in a devotional mood. You may choose to be silent that day as it preserves and increases prana. Muslims, Hindus, Buddhists, Sikhs, Jains, Christians and Jews all fast as a religious observance. You may even resolve to give up any bad habits on the day of your fast.

Breaking a Fast

How you break your fast is very important. There is a saying that goes, "Any fool can fast, but only a wise person will know how to break it." How you break your fast depends on the length of the fast and the type of fast. The general rule for breaking a liquid fast is to return to a normal diet very gradually. Start with any easily digestible fruit juices like watermelon, orange or sweet lemon. Drink this two or three times to begin with, then gradually include fresh fruits. This way you gradually get back to your normal diet.

Don't be in a hurry; otherwise, you can damage your digestive system. For each day of water fasting, there should be one day of recovery. If you do a three-day water fast, you should spend at least three days recovering before engaging in any intense physical or mental activity. Remember the very idea of fasting during the presence of an acute condition is to restore the impaired digestive mechanism to its healthy, natural function.

If you are breaking a mono-diet fast, it depends on how long you fasted for as to how long it should take to come off of it. In a mono-diet such as eating only kichari for only one day, it is no problem to eat your normal, healthy diet again the next day. If you have done fourteen to twenty eight days of kichari, it should be broken with easily digestible vegetable soups for a few days, gradually increasing the amount of vegetables over a week or so.

Who Should Fast?

Do not seek help from a conventional doctor for a condition that conventional medicine cannot treat, and do not rely on an alternative provider for a condition that conventional medicine can manage well.

– Dr.Andrew Weil M.D.

Almost everyone can gain great benefits from a fast. However, there are a few exceptions due to special circumstances in which fasting should be avoided. Fasting is still viewed as an "alternative" therapy as it is not recognized, prescribed or utilized by the majority of conventional Western doctors. Western medicine attempts to treat ailments and conditions primarily through invasive techniques. While many of these modern techniques are highly successful in treating some conditions, as well as saving lives, they fail miserably in prevention and successful treatment of numerous other health conditions. Fasting allows the body to *heal itself* in a way that harmoniously affects the whole organism. It allows for a rebalancing on all levels of our being and permits the innate cellular intelligence to emerge.

Conventional medicine benefits:

• Management of trauma better than any other system of medicine
• Diagnostics and treatment of numerous medical and surgical emergencies
• Treatment of acute bacterial infections with antibiotics
• Treatment of some parasitic and fungal infections
• Diagnostics of complex medical problems
• Replacement of damaged hips and knees
• Cosmetic and reconstructive surgery
• Diagnostics and correction of hormonal deficiencies

Conventional medicine may help the symptoms but is often unable to help eliminate the root cause of:

• Viral infections
• The majority of degenerative diseases
• The management of the majority of mental illness
• Most forms of allergy or autoimmune disease
• Psychosomatic illnesses

Who Should Not Fast?

• **Pregnant and nursing women.** Growing babies and their mothers need food to grow.

• **Infants and young children.** In the U.S. it is considered un-advisable to permit young children to fast; however, in Europe it is permissible if the child is obese and has chosen to fast of his/her own will and is supervised by a professional. Nevertheless, most of the traditional cultures of the world believed children are among the best candidates for fasting as their bodies and minds are pure and untainted by bad habits and the onslaught of the shadripus. There is a widespread misconception that the more growing children eat, the more healthy and strong they will be. What needs to be clearly realized is that it is not the amount of food eaten but the quality of digestion of nutritious food that determines the health, strength and growth of children.

• **Those who have a medical conditions.** Those with liver or kidney weakness, or those who are extremely frail, malnourished, anemic, or exhausted should not fast. Fasting is to be avoided by those with a depleted immune system, severely high blood pressure, blood-sugar disorders such as medication-dependent diabetes, hypoglycemia and hyperglycemia, or poor circulation with frequent fainting.

• **Those with eating disorders.** Those diagnosed with anorexia or bulimia shouldn't fast.

• **Those who have undergone surgery or a major illness.** There should be ample time given to rest and regenerate before attempting a fast. Fasting prior to a major surgery should also be avoided.

• **Those who are in fear.** Fear puts the mind in a negative state for fasting and can lead to an unpleasant experience. Strong emotions, such as fear and anxiety, are proven to alter the body's biochemistry and physiological processes. It can alter or impede certain bodily functions. When one is fasting, they should feel relaxed, confident and open to the positive changes fasting allows.

Types of Fasting:

1. Water Fasting

Water fasting is the most ancient and common form of fasting. This typically involves drinking nothing but water for a set period of time. Some people like to add a little lemon to the water for taste. A generally safe period of time for water fasting is one to three days.

The basics of water fasting are to drink 64-96 oz. (2-3 lt.) of pure water throughout the day. It is best to start the day by drinking 24-40 oz. (750ml-1.25 lt.) of warm water upon rising.

If you are in a tropical climate and fresh coconuts are available, coconut water may be used for the fast as well. It is Nature's most perfect water. Many find it quite easy to fast on coconut water as it provides deep cellular hydration and lots of nutrients. Coconut water contains simple sugars, electrolytes and minerals to replenish hydration levels within the body. In scientific studies, the cytokines (phytohormones that promote cell growth) in coconut water showed significant anti-aging, anti-carcinogenic and anti-thrombotic effects. Coconut water is composed of many naturally occurring bioactive enzymes such as acid phosphatase, catalase, dehydrogenase, diastase, peroxidase, RNA-polymerases and more. These enzymes substantially help the digestive and metabolic systems. While coconut water has a very light consistency, it has a rich composition of minerals like calcium, iron, manganese, magnesium and zinc. It contains more of these vitamins and minerals than fruits such as oranges and grapefruits. The water is also a valuable source of

B-complex vitamins such as riboflavin, niacin, thiamin, pyridoxine and folate. These are essential vitamins as the human body requires them from external sources. One may do a fast comprised of a combination of water and coconut water. With a one-day water fast, it is ideal that the last meal before the fast and the first meal after the fast is fresh fruit.

Water Types

There are numerous "types" of water available today. It is recommended to use the purest water available. This is a brief overview of the different "types" of water you can get. Choose what you feel best suits your needs. It is best to avoid buying water packaged in 'soft' plastic as the water typically leaches toxins from the bottle. Numerous water filtration systems are available at health food stores and on the internet that you can use at home.

• **Alkaline (pH alkaline 7.0 +).** Alkaline water helps to neutralize acid in the bloodstream, leading to increased oxygen levels as well as increased energy and metabolism. Water that is alkaline has antioxidant properties that help by counteracting free radicals. The antioxidants that are in a liquid form allow for quicker absorption into the system. The benefits of alkaline water are significantly clear since alkaline water has anti-aging and anti-diseases properties. It is also believed that pH-balanced water contains certain elements that will aid in developing cancer resistance. Alkaline water assists to lubricate the muscles and joints and to help prevent injuries. Alkaline water is the most hydrating of all waters. As dehydration can harm organs such as the heart and kidneys, alkaline water can be considered preventative medicine. There are numerous alkaline water systems available for home use.

• **Artesian (pH will vary).** Water obtained from a well that taps a confined aquifer, an underground layer of rock or sand that contains water.

• **Distilled (pH acid).** Water that has been boiled and then re-condensed from the steam that the boiling produces. Distillation kills microbes and removes minerals, giving water a flat taste. Distilled water is water that has first been turned into steam so that all of its impurities are left behind. Then through condensation, it is turned back into pure water. Some consider this the only truly pure water as it is the only water that is absolutely free from all contamination. Steam-distilled water is not good for long-term use, but it is beneficial for short-term cleansing as it binds to toxins and carries them out of the body.

• **Hard Water (pH acid).** Hard water is saturated with minerals like calcium, iron, magnesium and many other inorganic minerals. All water in lakes, rivers, on the ground and in deep wells is classified as hard water. While it is safe to drink, it is highly acidic and can create numerous health problems. Hard water can be easily "softened" or filtered to make it easier on the digestive system.

• **Natural Mineral (pH will vary).** Natural mineral water is usually obtained directly from underground sources protected from pollution risks. Natural mineral water is water of pristine purity. By law, natural mineral water must originate from a subterranean source that is protected from every possible contamination. Only water that has been officially approved and tested for purity may be labeled "natural mineral water." Before reaching this stage, it must pass about 200 separate analyses. Mineral water is groundwater that naturally contains at least 250 parts per million of dissolved solids. All minerals and other trace elements must be present in the water when it emerges at the source. It is packaged close to the point of emergence of the source to maintain purity.

• **P.S.W. (Tap Water) (pH high acid).** Public source water is also known as the municipal water supply or simply tap water. While tap water is generally safe to drink, it is heavily filtered and treated with chemicals to reduce parasite and bacterial presence. Tap water is usually not a natural product, especially in cities. Tap water may carry heavy chlorine residue to maintain microbiological safety during storage and transit through water mains, tanks and pipes that may not always be in the best of conditions. Tap water in large cities usually contains trace amounts of numerous pharmaceutical drugs and other damaging chemicals. The majority of tap water has been used in some capacity before, so it is recycled, re-treated and re-filtered before consumption.

• **Purified (pH acid).** Water from any source that has been treated to remove chemicals and pathogens according to standards set by the U.S. Pharmacopoeia. It must contain no more than 10 parts per million of dissolved solids. Distillation, deionization and reverse osmosis are all purification methods.

The five pranic factors

• **Reverse Osmosis (R.O.) (pH acid).** Reverse osmosis (RO) is a water purification technology that uses a semi-permeable membrane. This is a process that exposes water under pressure to a semi-permeable membrane with a very fine pore structure. Because most inorganic contaminants are of a larger molecular size than water, the membrane rejects certain contaminants, minerals and a large part of the water. A good R.O. system can remove contaminants such as arsenic, nitrates, sodium, copper, lead, some organic chemicals and the municipal additive fluoride. The one real health advantage to drinking R.O. water is that the process removes the unhealthy contaminants.

• **Sparkling (pH acid).** Water that contains carbon dioxide at an amount equal to what it contained when it emerged from its source. Carbon dioxide lost during the treatment process may be added back.

• **Spring (pH will vary, usually neutral or slightly alkaline depending on source).** Water derived from an underground formation from which water flows naturally to the Earth's surface. Spring water must be collected at the spring or through a borehole tapping the underground formation (aquifer) feeding the spring. Natural spring water has not passed through a community water system.

Juice Fasting

Juice fasting provides an incredible way to detox while increasing health and vitality. The nutritional benefits of fresh organic juices will help your body to heal, rebuild and detoxify waste products. Short, one to seven day juice fasts are of great benefit in cultivating a balanced state of health. Many naturopaths and nutritionists encourage juice fasting over water fasting. It is more gentle than water fasting, and it gives the body high-quality nutrients in an easily digestible, bioavailable form. The vitamins, minerals and enzymes in fresh juice are easily absorbed by the blood and do not burden the body's digestive system. Juice fasting also helps to acquire a taste for fresh, sattvic food and to become accustomed to increased vitality.

Both fruit and vegetable juices can be used. As per proper food combining rules, they shouldn't be mixed in the same drink. Canned, bottled and frozen juices are devoid of prana and should be avoided during a juice fast. Use the freshest, highest-quality, organic produce during a fast. Living foods such as raw juices have quite a potent nature. It is recommended that you dilute them by at least 1/4 (1 part water to 3 parts juice). Citrus juices may even be diluted in half. Three to five glasses (16 oz./480 ml.) of juice can be taken every day along with plenty of water, at least 64 oz. (2 lt.). As the nutrients break down quickly, fresh juice should be consumed right away and not stored for any length of time. Some great traditional juices used for fasting are apple, beet, cabbage, carrot, celery, citrus, cucumber, grape and "green drinks" from leafy greens, including wheat grass. Sample recipes are provided at the end of the book.

Master Cleanse Fasting

The Master Cleanse is a popular method of fasting or detoxification that is practiced worldwide. It is considered to be a relatively easy way of fasting. The ingredients are readily available all over the world, and it has enough calories to keep your energy level up. The Master Cleanse is composed of water with lemon juice, Grade B maple syrup and cayenne pepper. Grade B maple syrup provides nutrients and calories in the form of simple sugars. With the Master Cleanse, one doesn't enter into a full ketosis state like with water fasting. However, ketosis is not necessary for the purpose of detox and cleansing. Stanley Burroughs created the

Master Cleanse recipe in 1941 in his book called *The Master Cleanser*. In his book, ten days is the standard length of a Master Cleanse. However, it can be undertaken for various lengths of time.

Ayurveda does not necessarily agree with this method of fasting. It has a tendency to be aggravating to the doshas. Like with water or juice fasting, Master Cleanse can be safely used for a one to three day fast. If you are considering a longer version of this fast, please consult a health care professional first. It is included here for informational purposes only and not as a promotion.

Master Cleanse Recipe

   Water – 8oz. [1]
   Fresh Squeezed Lemon or Lime Juice – 2 TBS
   100% Pure Grade B or C Maple Syrup – 1-2 TBS
   Cayenne Pepper – 1/10 tsp.

You can premix a large quantity and store it in an airtight glass container. However, it is better if the lemon and cayenne pepper can be added fresh to each glass as their nutrients break down quickly. Drink 6-12 glasses per day.

---

[1] 1 ounce equals 30 milliliter.

If you choose to do a full ten-day Master Cleanse, take three to five days to transition back to normal foods. Start with several glasses of fruit juice on the first day. On the second day, you may take orange juice, vegetable broth and fresh fruit. On the third day, cooked veggies may be added. On the fourth day, you can return to a normal diet.

Partial Fasting

Yoga says that a person who eats only one meal a day is permanently fasting. Naturopathy calls this partial fasting. This means taking one meal a day between 12:00 and 2:00 p.m. each day. The rest of the day involves drinking plenty of water and fresh fruit or vegetables juices as well as herbal teas suitable for one's constitution. This means drinking 24-40 oz. (750 ml-1.25 lt.) of water upon rising as well as another 32-48 oz. (1-1.5 lt.) of total liquids throughout the day.

This may be too extreme for some constitutions or lifestyles. A milder version of this is to take the usual morning water followed by only a small piece of fruit in the morning and then a meal mid-day. Another way of doing a partial fast is on liquids mixed with protein powders. This may be suitable for those with active lifestyles or those who need to keep their energy levels up. One may use a vegan plant protein or whey protein that is organic, grass-fed and hormone and antibiotic-free. A typical serving ranges from 15-25 grams of protein per serving. It can be mixed in 16-32 oz. of pure water, coconut water or juice.

Mono-Diet

Some people maybe not feel ready to begin fasting using the previously mentioned methods. This may include people who have to do some moderate to strong physical labor. For such people, a mono-diet can still be of great assistance in the detoxification and healing process. It is also appropriate for those who wish to cleanse but cannot withdraw from demanding daily responsibilities. A mono-diet refers to eating a specific food for a period of time. This typically involves only eating fruits or vegetables for all meals one day a week or for up to three days.

Ayurveda often recommends a mono-diet of *Kichari* (mung dal and basmati rice cooked together). Kichari is a traditional Ayurveda dish and is the primary diet during *pancha karma* (Ayurvedic cleansing therapy- literally means 'five actions'). Kichari is a complete protein that's one of the easiest foods to digest. It is harmonizing for all doshas. It has a soothing and calming effect on the nervous system and helps to alleviate stress and remove toxicity from the digestive tract.

There is a recipe for kichari later in this book. Kichari and other mono-diet foods allow the digestive system a chance to regulate itself. It is the next best thing to a pure fast. For some people, it is actually safer and more balancing. A mono-diet may extend from one day to thirty days. As with any type of extended fast, professional advice is recommended.

Different fasts for different doshas

Not all doshas can or should be doing extensive fasting.

A vata dosha is light and dry to begin with, so they should not undertake fasting for more than a couple of days. In general, raw food or juicing is not great for a vata type as it easily cause them to become ungrounded. Most vata people should limit water/ juice fasts to one day a week if they are relatively healthy. For those who are weak or debilitated, juice/water fasts are not advised. However, for all vata people, a kichari mono-diet can help regulate the digestive system. Depending on personal needs, kichari can be taken for three to twenty-eight days.

A pitta type is stronger and can generally do more fasting. Pitta individuals can benefit from raw food fasts, juice fasting or even short water fasts. If a pitta person fasts for too long, they can become irritable and aggressive. This is a sign that it is time to end the fast. Pitta people also do great with kichari, fruit or vegetable mono- diets.

A kapha type is usually safe to do the most fasting and cleansing. Water should be taken warm or even with ginger. Kapha can easily do an extended fast under professional guidance.

People with all bodily constitutions should take into account the season and weather when choosing a time to fast. Fasting for long periods in the middle of a cold winter can prove to be more harmful than helpful. In general, a great time to fast is with the changing of the seasons: spring equinox, summer solstice, fall equinox and winter solstice. As fasting tends to cool down the body, in the cold season it is better to do a one-day fast that includes hot water or a mono-diet of kichari or steamed vegetables.

Chapter 17

Colon care

It is good for a seeker to purge the stomach at least twice a month. The accumulated feces in the intestines creates agitation and negativity in the mind. By purging, we clear not only the body but the mind as well.

– Amma

Ayurveda and Naturopathy acknowledge that health begins with the colon. Illness and disease begin with toxins in the colon and spread from there. In addition to fasting, one of the best things we can do to assure good health and a long life is to clean the colon. Please note that during a fast, colon cleansing is only really necessary if there are toxins built up in the colon.

There are a few excellent ways to clean the colon. There are many laxative herbal teas that can be taken in the evening before bed. There are traditional salt-water flushes as well as colonics and enemas. There are colon hydrotherapists available in most cities that can provide 'high colonics,' a machine-administered enema that injects large amounts of fluid high into the colon for cleansing purposes.

A gentle enema can easily be administered by oneself or with the assistance of a family member or close friend. There are various types of enemas used in traditional Naturopathy and Ayurveda. Ayurveda traditionally uses some form of medicated oil or other substance. While traditional Naturopathy also uses oil, it relies heavily on other liquids such as coffee, baking soda, herbal teas, wheatgrass juice, Epsom salt, Himalaya salt and sea salt. Remember that fasting in general promotes healthy bowel movements and that other means of colon cleansing should only be administered if the bowels are sluggish or overloaded with excess toxins.

Purgation or enemas are contraindicated in acute stages of fever, severe debilitation, very young or very old persons, weak digestion, wounds in the anus, prolapsed rectum, ulcerative colitis, appendicitis, congestive heart failure, diarrhea and very hard bowels.

Oral colon cleanse recipe

Different people's bodies respond differently to various cleansing methods. It is advisable to proceed with awareness and to be willing to adjust as necessary.

Colon care

Psyllium Husk and Bentonite Cleanse

Psyllium Husk - 1 tsp.

Bentonite Clay Powder - 1 tsp. or Liquid Bentonite Clay – 1 TBS

Water or Fresh Fruit Juice – 8 oz.

Mix the psyllium husk and bentonite clay in an empty glass or shaker cup and add the water. Shake or stir it briskly.

Drink immediately so that it does not thicken.

Drink another eight ounces of pure water or juice. Hydration is essential in cleansing.

This can be taken the night before a one-day juice fast or nightly if doing an extended fast. If there are a lot of toxins present, it can be taken two or three times a day for the period of the fast.

Triphala Tea

Triphala is composed of the dried fruits of amalaki, bibhitaki and haritaki (Terminalia Belerica, Terminalia Chebula and Emblica Officinalis). Triphala has been used for thousands of years to lower blood pressure, increasing HDL cholesterol and lowering LDL cholesterol. Triphala is also commonly used to regulate blood sugar and to promote weight loss. Triphala promotes healthy bacteria growth and restores pH balance of the G.I. tract.

To make a gentle triphala tea, use ½ to 1 tsp. of the powder. Put the powder into a cup, pour hot water over it and allow it to steep for five to ten minutes.

To make triphala as a laxative and bowel tonic, any of the following methods are effective ways to aid and regulate elimination:

Drink the tea, powder and all, before bedtime. To have a stronger elimination, boil ½ to 1 tsp. for three to five minutes then strain it before drinking. A cold infusion can be made by soaking one teaspoon of triphala in one cup of room-temperature water overnight. Drink it first thing in the morning on an empty stomach. If there is vata type constipation (dry) and triphala isn't work, adding a ¼ tsp. of licorice powder per ½ tsp. triphala will moisturize the colon.

Castor Oil:

Castor oil is a good, general treatment for constipation. It creates an overall healthy evacuation. An average dose is ½ - 1 ounce with a full glass of warm to hot water or juice such as cranberry juice, orange juice, prune juice or ginger juice.

Colon care

Aloe Vera Juice:

Taking aloe vera juice makes for a great purgation. The dosage may vary based on the individual. Dosage is anywhere from 1 ounce to 4 oz. Its health benefits reach far beyond just cleaning the colon. Aloe vera contains up to 19 amino acids, 20 minerals and 12 vitamins. Aloe vera's numerous healing benefits include:

1. Improves circulation
2. Regulates blood pressure
3. Promotes the healing of bones and joints
4. Strengthens the immune system
5. Defends the body against bacteria
6. Heals internal tissue damage
7. Heals ulcers
8. Helps to control stomach acid and maintains a balance in the stomach
9. Improves and eliminates constipation
10. Improves/regulates blood sugar levels
11. Reduces the itchiness of psoriasis
12. Detoxifies the body
13. Aids in digestion
14. Cleanses the colon
15. Assists in weight loss

Different types of enemas

Water Enema

A pure-water enema creates movement within the colon, encouraging the release of toxic waste. It stimulates nerve-reflex points within the colon that are connected to the rest of the body. The movement within the colon stimulates the movement and release of mucous from the lymphatic system. The water held within the colon is absorbed by the body and in turn improves overall hydration. On completion, there is usually a feeling of lightness.

Pure, filtered water – 32 oz. Warm water (just above body temperature- test with finger so as not to burn yourself!)

Administer the enema, hold as long as possible up to 30 minutes, then release.

Salt Enema

Himalayan or Dead Sea salt enemas create a relaxation of the smooth muscles of the intestinal tract and promote elimination of the colon's toxic material.

Using Himalayan or Dead Sea salts in an enema is a faster and safer way to achieve a cleansing than taking the salts orally. A salt solution will increase the amount

176

of water in the intestines because it draws water into the colon. This results in a more thorough cleansing of the colon. A salt enema is an overall good solution to use when suffering from constipation.

Salt Enema Recipe:

Pure water – 64 oz. (2 lt.) warm water
Himalaya or Dead Sea salt – 4 TBS

Add the salt to warm water and mix well until all salts are dissolved. Administer the solution and retain for a comfortable amount of time.

Coffee Enema

While it might seem strange to inject your morning coffee into your colon, coffee enemas are famous for their detoxification effects. The palmitates in coffee (kahweol and cafestol) enhance the action of glutathione S-transferase, a family of enzymes that play an essential role in the body's natural detoxification process. In addition to cleaning the colon, coffee helps to detoxify the liver and gall bladder as well. Coffee enemas do not pass through the digestive system and do not affect the body the same way as drinking coffee does. When coffee is administered rectally, the hepatic portal veins carry the caffeine directly to the liver. Coffee contains caffeine, theobromine and theophylline, substances that cause a dilation of the blood vessels and promote bile flow. Bile is the means through which the liver eliminates stored toxins. Bile (including toxic bile) is reabsorbed nine or ten times by the intestinal walls before it is eliminated through the colon. By using coffee enemas, one assists the elimination of the toxic bile from the body. The coffee enema is one of the most famous enemas due to its promising effects in alternative cancer treatment. Dr. Max Gerson used the coffee enema extensively in the 1940s for the treatment of cancer. There has been more recent research on the highly beneficial use of coffee enemas in cancer treatment through the work of Dr. Nicolas Gonzalez.

Coffee-Enema Recipe:

Organic, fair-trade coffee – 3 TBS

Pure, filtered water – 32 oz. (1 lt.)

Add the coffee to the water, boil for 3 minutes then reduce the heat and simmer on low for 15 minutes. Let the coffee cool to body temperature, filter and administer. Retain the enema for 15-20 minutes if possible.

Cautions and Considerations:

To make certain the cleansing is complete, you may want to administer another enema four to six hours later. This will remove any bile that happened to be released into the small intestine if there was any left over that was not eliminated in the first enema.

Use only organically grown coffee as commercial coffee is loaded with chemicals.

The coffee enema goes directly to the liver, and so do any chemicals that were used in the cultivation of that coffee.

It is recommended to avoid coffee enemas in the evening as some individuals can still experience side effects of caffeine. Those with sensitivity to caffeine should not take a coffee enema.

Lemon-Juice Enema

A lemon-juice enema eliminates excess feces and helps balance the pH levels in the colon. Relief from the discomfort and pain associated with colitis may be achieved by taking a lemon-juice enema on a weekly basis. Also, when used on a weekly basis, lemon-juice enemas provide relief from chronic constipation. A lemon-juice enema is more effective at cleansing the colon than a plain-water or saltwater enema.

Lemon-Juice Enema Recipe:

Freshly squeezed lemon juice – 2/3 cup
Warm, filtered water – 64 oz. (2 lt.)

Mix the water and lemon juice together, administer and retain for 15-20 minutes.

Salt and Baking Soda Enema

Baking soda is a completely alkaline substance. Using baking soda internally helps to neutralize acids, and as an enema, it is beneficial for people with conditions involving excess acidity. This enema can also help restore the acid-alkaline balance during illness. A salt and baking soda enema is useful for those suffering from colitis as it helps to prevent and heal ulcers in the colon caused by acidity.

Salt and Soda Enema Recipe:

Himalaya or Dead Sea salt – 2 tsp.
Baking soda – 1 TBS
Warm, filtered water – 64 oz. (2 lt.)

Mix the salt and soda until dissolved. Administer and retain the enema for a minimum of ten minutes.

Aloe Vera Enema

An aloe vera enema provides relief for inflammatory conditions within the digestive system. Aloe vera is an excellent moisturizer and soother. When used in an enema, it has an anti-inflammatory effect on the mucosa of the colon.

Aloe Vera Enema Recipe:

Pure, filtered warm water – 32 oz. (1 lt.)

Whole-leaf aloe vera juice – Quantity depends on desired strength of the enema:

Mild: 1-2 TBS

Medium: 3-5 TBS

Strong: 6-10 TBS

Wheatgrass Enema

A wheatgrass enema is similar to a coffee enema except wheatgrass is loaded with nutrients and oxygen. It is both cleansing and nutritive. Wheatgrass enemas are an excellent way to balance pH. They have been used for over 50 years in curing the numerous ailments associated with a toxic liver and colon as well as immune deficiencies. Wheatgrass provides an abundance of energy due to the vitamins entering directly into the bloodstream.

Wheatgrass Enema Recipe:

Pure, warm water – 64 oz. (2 lt.)

Wheatgrass juice – ½ -1 oz. (15-30 ml.) or wheat-grass juice powder ½-1 tsp.
Mix together and apply the enema. Hold 10-15 minutes.
You can also do an implant. This means you take 3-6 oz. (180-360 ml.) of wheatgrass juice, administer it to the colon and hold as long as possible. This is a highly nutritive tonic.

Wheatgrass Nutrition

One oz. (30 ml.) of freshly squeezed wheatgrass juice is equivalent in nutritional value to 2.2 lbs. (1kg.) of dark leafy green vegetables.

Wheatgrass contains over 90 minerals, including high concentrations of the most alkaline minerals: potassium, calcium, magnesium and sodium.

It contains the essential enzymes: protease (assists in protein digestion), cytochrome oxidase (a powerful antioxidant), amylase (facilitates digestion), lipase (a fat-splitting enzyme), transhydrogenase (strengthens the heart muscle) and superoxide dismutase or SOD (found in all body cells and known for its ability to reduce the effects of radiation and slow cellular aging).

One teaspoon of wheatgrass powder, weighing 3.5 grams, is equal in nutrition to a spinach salad weighing 50 grams.

Wheatgrass contains 19 amino acids.

Wheatgrass juice helps the body to build red blood cells, which carry oxygen to every cell. By increasing the oxygenation, the body can help offset environmental pollutants like smog and carbon monoxide.

How to Do an Enema

The enema introduces liquid, by means of an enema bag, through the anus that leads to the rectum and colon. Complete enema-bag kits may be purchased at most pharmacies, drug stores, grocery stores or natural food stores. A typical enema kit is composed of an enema bag, an enema tap or flow-control valve, two nozzles (one for the anus and one for the vagina) and a tubing apparatus. There are also enema-bucket kits available via the internet.

Instructions

• Prepare the area where you are going to do the enema with suitable protective material, i.e. a towel, warm compress, etc.

• Make up the liquid enema.

• Close the enema tap and fill the enema bag/bucket with the enema fluid.

• Hang the enema bag/bucket up so that it is positioned about three feet above the position you are going to lie or kneel in.

• Place the enema nozzle into a small cup and open the enema tap to allow the release of any air that may be trapped in the enema tube into the cup. Close the enema tap.

• Lubricate the anal area with oil (sesame, coconut, ghee work well).

• Get into a comfortable position to receive the enema (on your back, side or kneeling). For enemas targeting the liver (coffee) it is better to lie on the right side. This position facilitates the passage of the enema fluid to the liver.

• Insert 1-2 inches of the enema nozzle gently into the anus.

• Open the valve to allow the fluid to enter.

• Massage the abdomen or apply a warm compress.

• Hold the enema for the specified time.

• Upon completion, move to the toilet to expel the enema.

Enema Tips

If doing the enema feels too difficult, try doing the enema whilst submerged in a warm bath as this will help to relax the abdominal muscles. The quantity of fluid may need to be adjusted to compensate for difficulties in holding it. Never do an enema when hungry.

Chapter 18

Dry-skin brushing for health and detox

Dry-skin brushing helps eliminate dead-skin cells and toxins, helping to create healthier, revitalized skin. Skin brushing isn't a new practice. Numerous historical Ayurvedic and Chinese medicine texts refer to massaging the skin with various instruments including sticks, sand and rocks.

When detoxing through fasting, opening the pores of the skin helps to facilitate the elimination of toxins. The skin is one of the major eliminative organs, and it is estimated that a third of the body's toxins and waste materials are excreted through the skin during a fast.

The rasa dhatu (lymphatic system) plays a significant role in the detoxification of the body. When the waste materials leave the cells, they are carried out by the blood or lymph. While the blood has the heart to pump it quickly throughout the body, the lymph moves significantly slower, powered either by small muscle tissues lining the lymph vessels or by the movements of the larger, surrounding skeletal muscles. When the lymph is carrying a large amount of toxins, it contains more mucus to hold those toxins in suspension. This mucus thickens and slows the movement of the lymphatic system. Stimulating the lymphatic system during fasting helps the body to eliminate the toxins more easily.

The benefits of dry-skin brushing

• Enhancing blood flow to the skin's surface
• Stimulating the lymphatic, nervous, circulatory and glandular systems
• Opening of the pores by removing dead skin cells, allowing the skin to breathe better and perspire freely
• Stimulating the oil glands on the skin, allowing more of the body's natural oil to reach the surface
• Improving skin tone
• Alleviating any cleansing reactions from fasting, such as headaches
• Giving an overall invigorating effect physically and mentally

Chapter 19

Recipes

The sun, with all those planets revolving around it that are dependent on it, can still ripen a bunch of grapes as if it had nothing else in the universe to do.

— Galileo

Here some examples of recipes that can be used for fasting. Be creative and come up with your own delicious concoctions. Remember food-combining laws; fruit and vegetables don't go together.

If you are using the metric system for measuring, 1 oz. = 30 ml. and 1 qt. = 1 lt.

For any and all liquid recipes, the following ingredients may be added to any of the recipes:

Fresh Ginger Juice: 1-2 oz.

Fresh Cilantro (Coriander Leaf) Juice: 1-2 oz.

Cayenne Pepper Powder: a pinch

Lemon-Ginger-Honey Water:

Pure Water – 32 oz.

Ginger – 1 inch (chopped)

Lemon Juice – 1 -2 oz.

Raw Honey – 1-2 TBS

Chop the ginger into small pieces and boil for 5-7 minutes. Let the ginger steep for 15-30 minutes. Strain the ginger and add the honey and lemon.

Green Water:

Pure Water – 32 oz.
Wheatgrass Juice 1 oz. or ½ tsp. powder
Open-Cell/Broken-Wall Chlorella – ½ tsp.
Organic Spirulina – ½ tsp.
Aloe Vera Juice – 2 oz.

Juices

Aloe Pomegranate:

Whole-Leaf Aloe Vera Juice – 2 oz.

Pomegranate – 4 oz. (If pomegranate juice is not available, this can be made by using 1 oz. pomegranate juice concentrate, which is available in most health food stores or on the internet.)

Coconut Water or Pure Water – 8 oz.

Apple Tonic:

Apple – 8 oz.
Apple Cider Vinegar – 1 oz.
Aloe Vera Juice – 1 oz.

Antioxidant Tonic:

    Red Grape – 6 oz.
    Blueberry – 2 oz.
    Cherry – 2 oz.
    Pomegranate – 2 oz.
    Aloe Vera Juice – 2 oz.

Wheatgrass Juice:

    Pure Water or Coconut Water – 8 oz.
    Fresh Wheatgrass Juice - 1 oz. or ½ tsp. Wheatgrass Juice Powder

Agni Tonic:

    Pure Water – 8 oz.
    Ginger – 2 oz.
    Raw Honey – ½ tsp.

Ginger Lemonade:

    Pure Water – 10 oz.
    Lemon – 4 oz.
    Ginger – 2 oz.
    Raw Honey – ½ tsp.

4-C Tonic:

    Carrot – 8 oz.
    Celery – 4 oz.

Cucumber – 4 oz.

Cilantro – 2 oz.

Add ginger juice and cayenne pepper for warmth!

Blood Tonic:

Beet Root – 6 oz.

Burdock Root – 4 oz.

Red Cabbage – 4 oz.

Celery – 2 oz.

Ginger – 1 oz.

Cayenne Pepper – 1/8 tsp.

Alkaline Tonic:

Carrot – 8 oz.

Beet – 4 oz.

Celery – 4 oz.

Red Cabbage – 2 oz.

Energy Tonic:

Carrot – 12 oz.

Garlic – 2 cloves

Parsley – 1 handful

Anti-Inflammatory Tonic:

Carrot – 7 oz.

Celery – 4 oz.

Broccoli – 3 oz.
Asparagus – 2 oz.
Parsley – 1 handful
Cilantro – 1 handful
Ginger – 1 inch
Turmeric – 1 inch

Immune Booster:

Beet Root – 6 oz.
Spinach – 4 oz.
Celery – 3 oz.
Carrot – 4 oz.
Kale – 2 oz.
Burdock Root – 2 oz.
Ginger – 1-2 inches

Getting Green:

Celery – 6 oz.
Spinach – 2 oz.
Kale – 2 oz.
Cilantro – 2 oz.
Parsley – 2 oz.
Cucumber -2 oz.
Broccoli – 2 oz.

Summer Breeze:

Cucumber – 12 oz.
Celery – 4 oz.
Cilantro – 2 oz.
Mint – 1 handful
Juice the cucumber, celery and cilantro, add the mint and juice to a blender and mix for 30 seconds.

Apple Lemon Mint:

Apple – 12 oz.
Lemon – 4 oz.
Mint – 1 handful
Juice the apple and lemon, add the mint and juice to a blender and mix for 30 seconds.

Coconut Dream:

Coconut Water – 8 oz.
Orange – 4 oz.
Pineapple – 4 oz.

Perfectly Peachy:

Coconut Water – 8 oz.
Peach – 6 oz.
Orange – 2 oz.

Citrus Bliss:

> Grapefruit – 8 oz.
> Orange – 4 oz.
> Lemon – 2 oz.
> Apple – 2 oz.

Grape Delight:

> Red Grape – 10 oz.
> Apple – 4 oz.
> Cherry – 2 oz.
> Lemon 1 oz.

Berry Good:

> Apple – 6 oz.
> Blueberry – 4 oz.
> Blackberry – 2 oz.
> Pear – 2 oz.
> Kiwi – 2 oz.

Aloha Sunrise:

> Coconut Water – 6 oz.
> Orange – 6 oz.
> Pineapple – 4 oz.
> Kiwi – 2 oz.

Pineapple Paradise:

Water – 8 oz.
Pineapple – 4 oz.
Ginger – 2 oz.
Lemon – 1 oz.
Mint – a handful
Raw Honey – ½ tsp.

Juice all the ingredients except the mint and honey. Add the juice, mint and honey to a blender and mix for 30 seconds.

Kichari (Serves: 4)

Ingredients:
Mung Beans - 2 cups
Basmati Rice - 1 cup
Water - 6 cups
Ghee - 2 TBS
Sea Salt – 1 tsp.
Fine-Ground Black Pepper Powder - ½ tsp.
Ginger Powder – ½ tsp.
Hing (asafetida) – 1/8 tsp.
Cumin Powder – 1 tsp.
Coriander Powder - 1 tsp.
Turmeric Powder - 1 tsp.
Fresh Cilantro, Finely Chopped – 1 cup

Instructions:

Soak the mung beans and basmati rice for several hours; then rinse well until the water runs clear. Bring 8 cups of water to a rapid boil. Add the mung beans and rice, bring back to a boil and reduce the temperature to medium and cook for 15 minutes. Keep it covered and stir every 3 minutes. After about half an hour, cook the ghee and spices on a low to medium heat in a saucepan for about five minutes. Add to the kichari. Cook for another 5-10 minutes. Remove from heat, add the cilantro and cover. Let it sit for 10 minutes before serving. You may add a tablespoon of plain yogurt to your personal serving. If you prefer the kichari spicy, you may add half a teaspoon of cayenne pepper or a couple of finely chopped chili peppers to the spices when cooking.

*Aum brahmarpanam brahma havir
brahmagnau brahmana hutam brahmaiva
tena gantavyam brahma karma samadhina*

Brahman is the oblation. Brahman is the
food offering. By Brahman it is offered into
the fire of Brahman. Brahman is that which
is to be attained by complete absorption
(samadhi) in the action of Brahman.

Bhagavad Gita, 4:24

Chapter 20

The goal of life

*Our body is perishable. Only the soul is permanent.
This is a rented body. We will be asked to leave at
any time. Before that, we should look for a place in a
permanent abode. Then, when we leave the body, we
will move to that permanent abode, the eternal house
of God. No one brings anything into this world, nor
does anyone take anything with him when he leaves.*

— Amma

Knowing that we are in "rented" bodies, we sense that
there must be some higher purpose or goal for us than
to simply enjoy the material comforts and pleasures of
a temporary existence. Ayurveda and yoga state that
there are four goals or desires in life that are considered
legitimate or worthwhile. These are referred to as the
purusharthas and are considered applicable to every
human being. These universal, basic desires are at the
heart of all other desires.

The four goals or desires identified in the *shastras*
(Vedic scriptures) are *kama, artha, dharma* and *moksha*.
All beings pursue one or all of these goals. Once a goal

has been identified, we must contemplate the right means and then work to attain it. The goal should be clear, cherished and sought with intensity and awareness. The degree to which we are seeking any of these four goals determines the balance and harmony we keep in life as well as the success we will achieve. The first three are catalysts for the fourth and ultimate goal of *moksha* (Self-realization). In order to attain any of these goals, we need to be strong, healthy and filled with vitality and love. We need a healthy body as well as a healthy heart and clear mind. Cleansing and fasting are the strongest appeal to the human being's natural powers of healing, on both a physical and spiritual level.

The four goals of life

1. *Kama* (desire): Kama means satisfying legitimate desires with the assistance of one's possessions (artha).
2. *Artha* (wealth): Artha means the accumulation of wealth or possessions while fulfilling one's duties (dharma).
3. *Dharma* (career/life path): In addition to one's career or work, dharma means the fulfillment of one's duties to society. Ideally, one's career and societal duties are in alignment with one another.

4. *Moksha* (liberation): Moksha is Self-realization and the realization that there is more to life than duties, possessions and desires (dharma, artha, kama).

Kama

Translated literally as "desire," kama is the achievement of one's personal aspirations. All ambitions and desires, including lust, are considered kama; however, on a deeper level, kama represents the innate urge to attain one's aspiration.

For most creatures, enjoyment is the essence of their existence. Everyone wants to be happy and free from suffering. However, in the world today, most people seek happiness from external things. Real, lasting, un-fluctuating happiness comes only from deep within one's Self, and not from external objects. External objects do serve valid purposes, but one should understand their proper place in life.

For example, many people in the world today crave sexual satisfaction; this desire guides many of their decisions and actions. Eventually, one must realize that the body and the world will inevitably perish. The true source of happiness lies within. This doesn't mean we shouldn't enjoy the objects of the world; it simply means that we need to understand their transient nature and let go of our attachment to those things. It is the attachment to external objects that is the cause of our suffering. Amma wants us to remember: "*Nothing in this material world is everlasting. Everything can go at anytime. Therefore, live in this world with the alertness of a bird perched on a dry twig. The bird knows that the twig can break at any time.*"

Artha

Artha means wealth or prosperity. It refers to the accumulation of wealth. We need a certain amount of wealth to live our lives. Our basic necessities include clothing, food, shelter and medicine when we are sick. Money represents a means of attaining resources. It facilitates the fulfillment of our desires and duties and helps bring about a sense of security. Wealth essentially allows us to function comfortably in life.

One's attitude toward money and work should be properly considered. If we are selfless and share what blessings we have with others, then there will always be enough for the whole world. If we hoard wealth, then people will go without and suffer. The universe is compassionate. Mother Earth is compassionate. She will always provide for her children if her bounty is not abused.

The goal of life

The sage Sri Adi Shankaracharya wrote in the *Vivekachudamani* (The Crest Jewel of Discrimination), "There is no hope of immortality by means of riches – such indeed is the declaration of the Vedas. Hence it is clear that works cannot be the cause of liberation."

If we are fortunate enough to have accumulated some wealth and we regularly donate a portion of our earnings to charitable causes that alleviate suffering, then we are performing a form of selfless service (Karma Yoga). Amma says, "*There is a difference between buying medicine to relieve your own pain and going out to get medicine for someone else. The latter shows a loving heart.*" The poverty of countries such as India is astounding. People suffer because they can't even afford a ten-rupee painkiller to alleviate a headache. Some people even die because they can't afford a three-dollar antibiotic. If we use a portion of our income to help such people, our lives will become blessed. When we serve selflessly, we start to feel the presence of the Divine blossoming within our hearts.

Dharma

Dharayati iti dharma means "that which sustains all." Dharma refers to right conduct and a righteous way of living in the world. Dharma can simply refer to our career or vocation, but it can also refer to how we live in the world. Following the path of right conduct and living a life of harmony and love is the real dharma. In its highest sense, dharma means the ultimate way or the natural law or way of things. Just as it is the dharma of the sun to shine and the dharma of the planets to revolve around the sun, humans have a dharma to follow. When followed carefully and with awareness, dharma will carry us across the ocean of samsara. To follow one's dharma is to surrender to the cosmic flow and natural law of the universe. The true role of spirituality is to reveal to each individual his or her unique dharma. However, at present, the involvement of the ego often relegates dharma to dogma and ritual. Dharma is much more than religion. It transcends all castes, limited viewpoints and philosophies. It is a way of life that enables peaceful co-existence with others and is conducive to the attainment of all our worldly and spiritual goals. The way each of us manifests dharma is unique. Mark Twain wrote, "Always do right. This will gratify some and astonish the rest." Everyone has unique talents for a specific reason. Amma says, "*You cannot simply adopt any path that you feel like. Each one will have a path, which they followed in the previous birth. Only if that path is followed will one progress in one's practice."*

If we put forth self-effort, God's grace will soon follow. Part of this effort involves looking within and finding our own path, our dharma. It is our responsibility to ourselves, to the world and to all of creation to allow our talents to be manifested in the world. The world is God's beautiful creation, and each person has a role to play in it. Playing our role in the world's perfection is the pinnacle of dharma, and in order to do so, we must not act blindly or apathetically. When each of us follows our individual and universal dharma, truth and righteousness will be restored to the world.

Nature is a huge flower garden. The animals, birds, trees, plants and people are the garden's fully blossomed flowers of diverse colors. The beauty of this garden is complete only when all of these exist as a unity, thereby spreading the vibrations of love and oneness. Let us work together to prevent these diverse flowers from withering away so that the garden may remain eternally beautiful.

– Amma

Moksha

Moksha means "freedom from the bonds of ignorance." The jiva can merge with Atman while living in the world. Moksha is complete freedom from the cycles of birth, death and rebirth; it is Self-realization. It is the freedom from all limitations of the mind, from limitations of time and space and from the dependence on artha and kama. Moksha is the realization of our Self as Brahman. This alone is Enlightenment. Anyone can reach this goal. Amma says, *"It is possible to reach your spiritual goal while leading a family life, provided you remain detached like a fish in muddy water. Perform your duties toward your family as your duty toward God. In addition to your husband or wife, you should have a friend – and that should be God."*

The first three purusharthas are outer goals, whereas the desire for moksha is an inner goal and the true purpose of life. Through knowledge of the impermanent, the desire for the permanent awakens. Eventually the desire for name, fame and wealth falls away. One does not have to give these things up; one only has to dissolve the attachment to and identification with them. This natural dissolution of old attachments is the first step toward renunciation of the materially focused life in order to reach the goal of moksha. Allowing these attachments and false identifications to fall away is real knowledge. Knowing that nothing is ours and all will pass in time awakens the discerning mind to the temporality of existence.

Amma knows the nature of each of our minds in relation to renunciation. She eloquently explains, "The word 'renunciation' scares some people. Their attitude is that if contentment can come only through giving up, then it is better not to be content. They wonder how they can lead a contented life without wealth, without a beautiful house, a nice car, a wife or husband, without all the conveniences and comforts of life. Without all these, life would be impossible; it would be hell, they think. But do you know anyone whose possessions make them really happy and content? People who look for happiness in life's many conveniences and comforts are the most miserable ones. The more wealth and comforts one has, the more worries and problems one will have. The more one desires, the more one will feel discontent because desires are endless. The chain of greed and selfishness continues to lengthen. It is an endless chain."

Health and Consciousness
through Fasting and Cleansing

When considering the four goals of life, dharma should always come first. We must try to establish our lives in righteousness. Our actions should be motivated by love and compassion instead of selfishness. Then, the proper use of artha and kama will manifest of their own accord. Through life experience, dispassion will arise, and the mind will turn inward. Lasting happiness will come from this inward awareness of the Self.

Ayurveda says that if we can follow these principles, then we can live harmonious, disease-free, healthful lives. Also, if we sincerely follow these guidelines, then we will assist in the restoration of harmony in the world. Sri Adi Shankaracharya said, "What greater fool is there than the one who, having obtained a rare human body, neglects to achieve the real end of this life?"

The ultimate goal of life, Self-realization, should become our primary focus. This precious human birth must not be wasted on sense pleasures and material pursuits alone. Instead, let us use this life to get free from the cycles of birth and death. Now is the only time there is. Turn inward and uncover the truth and beauty that remain hidden deep within.

Ayurveda, Naturopathy, yoga and fasting are invaluable tools that will help us on this journey. When the body and mind have been purified, we will see clearly the nature of the universe and the Self. We must put forth effort for grace to flow. We must strengthen our hearts and minds to be unwavering from the goal. May Amma's grace and love ever bless us.

Let us stand together and show the world that compassion, love and concern for our fellow beings have not completely vanished from the face of this earth. Let us build a new world of peace and harmony by remaining deeply rooted in the universal values that have nourished humanity since time immemorial. Let us say goodbye to war and brutality forever, reducing them to the stuff of fairytales. Let us be remembered in the future as the generation of peace.

– Amma

Book Catalog
By Author

Sri Mata Amritanandamayi Devi

108 Quotes On Faith
108 Quotes On Love
Compassion, The Only Way To Peace:
    Paris Speech
Cultivating Strength And Vitality
Living In Harmony
May Peace And Happiness Prevail:
    Barcelona Speech
May Your Hearts Blossom:
    Chicago Speech
Practice Spiritual Values And Save The
    World: Delhi Speech
The Awakening Of Universal Motherhood:
    Geneva Speech
The Eternal Truth
The Infinite Potential Of Women:
    Jaipur Speech
Understanding And Collaboration
    Between Religions
Unity Is Peace: Interfaith Speech

Swami Amritaswarupananda Puri

Ammachi: A Biography
Awaken Children, Volumes 1-9
From Amma's Heart
Mother Of Sweet Bliss
The Color Of Rainbow

Swami Jnanamritananda Puri

Eternal Wisdom, Volumes 1-2

Swami Paramatmananda Puri

Dust Of Her Feet
On The Road To Freedom Volumes 1-2
Talks, Volumes 1-6

Swami Purnamritananda Puri

Unforgettable Memories

Swami Ramakrishnananda Puri

Eye Of Wisdom
Racing Along The Razor's Edge
Secret Of Inner Peace
The Blessed Life
The Timeless Path
Ultimate Success

Swamini Krishnamrita Prana

Love Is The Answer
Sacred Journey
The Fragrance Of Pure Love
Torrential Love

M.A. Center Publications

1,000 Names Commentary
Archana Book (Large)
Archana Book (Small)
Being With Amma
Bhagavad Gita
Bhajanamritam, Volumes 1-6
Embracing The World
For My Children
Immortal Light
Lead Us To Purity
Lead Us To The Light
Man And Nature
My First Darshan
Puja: The Process Of Ritualistic
    Worship
Sri Lalitha Trishati Stotram

Amma's Websites

AMRITAPURI—Amma's Home Page
Teachings, Activities, Ashram Life, eServices, Yatra, Blogs and News
http://www.amritapuri.org

AMMA (Mata Amritanandamayi)
About Amma, Meeting Amma, Global Charities, Groups and Activities and Teachings
http://www.amma.org

EMBRACING THE WORLD®
Basic Needs, Emergencies, Environment, Research and News
http://www.embracingtheworld.org

AMRITA UNIVERSITY
About, Admissions, Campuses, Academics, Research, Global and News
http://www.amrita.edu

THE AMMA SHOP—Embracing the World® Books & Gifts Shop
Blog, Books, Complete Body, Home & Gifts, Jewelry, Music and Worship
http://www.theammashop.org

IAM—Integrated Amrita Meditation Technique®
Meditation Taught Free of Charge to the Public, Students, Prisoners and Military
http://www.amma.org/groups/north-america/projects/iam-meditation-classes

AMRITA PUJA
Types and Benefits of Pujas, Brahmasthanam Temple, Astrology Readings, Ordering Pujas
http://www.amritapuja.org

GREENFRIENDS
Growing Plants, Building Sustainable Environments, Education and Community Building
http://www.amma.org/groups/north-america/projects/green-friends

FACEBOOK
This is the Official Facebook Page to Connect with Amma
https://www.facebook.com/MataAmritanandamayi

DONATION PAGE
Please Help Support Amma's Charities Here:
http://www.amma.org/donations

CPSIA information can be obtained
at www.ICGtesting.com
Printed in the USA
LVOW13s0804230517
535206LV00007B/6/P